NOTRE DAME FOOTBALL
YESTERDAY & TODAY ™

MARTY STRASEN
FOREWORD BY LOU HOLTZ

WEST
SIDE
PUBLISHING

Marty Strasen is a senior editor for *The Tampa Tribune* and TBO.com in Tampa, Florida. He has authored or been a contributing writer on several sports books, including *The Best Book of Basketball Facts and Stats* and *Dark Horses and Underdogs*. A 1989 Notre Dame graduate, Strasen had the honor of covering the Fighting Irish for the student newspaper during the 1988 national championship season.

Lou Holtz established himself as one of the most successful college football coaches of all time. In his 11 seasons at Notre Dame, he racked up a record of 100–30–2, second only to the legendary Knute Rockne in all-time wins at the university. He also led the Fighting Irish to a consensus national championship in 1988, nine straight bowl games, and a 23-game winning streak. Currently, Holtz serves as a college football analyst for ESPN.

Factual verification by Nathan Rush

Special thanks to collectors Jim Augustine, John Augustine, and Andrew Augustine, who fulfilled a lifelong dream when they opened Augie's Locker Room in July 2007. Located near the Notre Dame campus, Augie's showcases their passion for Notre Dame football and sports memorabilia. Part museum, part sports collectibles store, Augie's houses one of the largest Knute Rockne collections in the country and is a place that every avid fan of the Fighting Irish should visit.

We would also like to thank Charles Lamb and Elizabeth Hogan from the Notre Dame Archives; Carol Copley, Michael Bertsch, and John Heisler from the Notre Dame Athletics Department; Jan Partain from Lou Holtz's office; and Notre Dame alumni Trevor Cickovski and Richard McConnell.

Yesterday & Today is a trademark of West Side Publishing.

West Side Publishing is a division of Publications International, Ltd.

Louis Weber, CEO
Publications International, Ltd.
7373 North Cicero Avenue
Lincolnwood, Illinois 60712

Permission is never granted for commercial purposes.

ISBN-13: 978-1-4127-1506-5
ISBN-10: 1-4127-1506-7

Manufactured in China.

8 7 6 5 4 3 2 1

Library of Congress Control Number: 2008923001

Front cover: **University of Notre Dame Archives**

Back cover: ***Sports Illustrated*/John Biever**

AP Images: 24 (left), 26 (top right), 80 (bottom left), 84, 120, 125, 127 (right), 138 (right), 143 (left), 149; **Courtesy of Augie's Locker Room:** Jim Augustine, John Augustine & Andrew Augustine, 27 (top left, top center, top right & bottom right), 29 (bottom left), 31 (left), 33 (left center, center & bottom left), 46 (right), 47 (top left, bottom left & bottom right), 49, 53 (top left), 64 (top center & bottom left), 71 (top right), 78 (bottom left), 79 (right center & bottom left), 83 (right), 86 (bottom left & bottom right), 98 (top left & top right), 99 (top left, bottom left & bottom right), 103 (right), 104 (bottom right), 107 (top & left center), 117 (left center), 132 (top right), 135 (right), 137 (top right), 140 (bottom left); **Courtesy of *Blue and Gold Illustrated:*** 146 (bottom right); **Chicago History Museum:** SDN-069606, 40 (bottom); **Trevor Cickovski Collection:** 150 (top right & bottom left); **Getty Images:** 29 (bottom center), 47 (top right), 73 (top), 82 (bottom), 83 (left), 91 (left), 118, 119 (right), 124 (left), 135 (left), 138 (left), 139, 142, 143 (right), 145 (left); **Courtesy of Lou Holtz:** 6, 9; **Jennifer Huston Photography:** 115 (bottom right), 150 (top left); **Lighthouse Imaging:** Michael & Susan Bennett, 105, 145 (right); **Richard McConnell Collection:** 67 (bottom center); **PIL Collection:** 14 (bottom center), 45, 46 (left); **Courtesy of Tony Roberts:** 146 (top right); ***Sports Illustrated:*** James Drake, 91 (right), Simon Bruty, 113; **Marty Strasen Collection:** 29 (bottom right), 71 (bottom right), 79 (top left, top right & left center), 122 (top left), 123; *The Arizona Republic:* 123 (top left & top right); **University of Notre Dame:** 147; **University of Notre Dame Archives:** 3, 7, 10, 11, 12, 13, 14 (top & bottom left), 15 (bottom), 16, 17, 18, 19, 20, 21, 22, 23, 24 (right), 25, 26 (top left & bottom), 27 (bottom left), 28, 29 (top left, top center & top right), 30, 31 (right), 32, 33 (top left, top right & right center), 34, 35, 36, 37 (right), 38, 39 (top, bottom left & bottom right), 40 (top), 41, 42, 43, 44, 45, 48, 49, 50, 51, 52, 53 (top right, bottom center & bottom right), 54, 55, 56, 57, 58, 59, 60, 61, 62, 63, 64 (top left, top right & bottom right), 65, 66, 67 (top right), 68, 69, 70, 72, 73 (bottom left & bottom right), 74, 75, 76, 77, 78 (top left, top center, top right, bottom center & bottom right), 80 (bottom right), 81, 82 (top), 85, 86 (top left, top center & top right), 87, 88, 89, 90, 92, 93, 94, 95, 96, 97, 98 (top center & bottom left), 99 (top right & left center), 100, 101 (right), 102, 103, 104 (left & top right), 105, 106, 107 (bottom), 108, 110, 111, 112, 114, 115 (left & top right), 116, 117 (top right & right center), 119 (left), 121, 122 (bottom left), 124 (right), 126, 128, 129, 130, 131, 132 (top left & bottom left), 133 (top left & bottom left), 134, 136, 137 (top left & bottom), 140 (top left), 141 (top center & left center), 144, 146 (top left & bottom left), 148, 151, 152; **University of Notre Dame Athletics Department:** 15 (top), 37 (left), 71 (top left & bottom left), 98 (bottom right), 101 (left), 122 (top right), 127 (left), 132 (bottom right), 133 (top right), 140 (top right & bottom center), 141 (top left, top right & bottom right)

Memorabilia Photography: Warling Studios/Brian Warling

A statue of the Virgin Mary atop the Golden Dome is instantly recognizable as the foremost symbol of the University of Notre Dame.

CONTENTS

Game Day   15

Knute Rockne   24

Notre Dame Nostalgia   64

All-Americans of the Era   92

Lou Holtz   120

Game Day   145

FOREWORD
BY LOU HOLTZ

My first knowledge of the University of Notre Dame came in 1943 when I attended St. Aloysius School in East Liverpool, Ohio. There we were taught by the Sisters of Notre Dame, who emphasized that every young Catholic should aspire to attend the University of Notre Dame, or at least cheer for the school. Every day at noon, recess, and dismissal we paraded out to the greatest song ever written, the "Notre Dame Victory March."

My father, grandfather, and uncles were all fans of the Fighting Irish. Because of the respect and love I had for them, I soon became a Notre Dame addict as well. I read everything I could about the Fighting Irish and listened to their games every Saturday afternoon. From 1946 to 1949, Notre Dame never lost a game. I thought that was the way college football was supposed to be: Notre Dame always wins.

Notre Dame's rich tradition and commitment to excellence are second to none. Following are some of the aspects that make that tradition so special.

Success

The success of Notre Dame on the football field is unprecedented. Notre Dame has won more national championships than any other school and has the second most victories among all colleges. Typically, the Fighting Irish are among the top ten football teams in the country. Yes, the team has some low spots in its history, but they are few and rare. You always expect Notre Dame to rise to the occasion and somehow find a way to win.

Coaches

No school has had more great coaches at their institution than Notre Dame. Probably the greatest was Knute Rockne, who was perhaps the most influential coach in the history of college football. As an end for the Fighting Irish, he worked with quarterback Gus Dorais to perfect the forward pass, which was legal but seldom used. Their talents led the 1913 Irish to an undefeated season, including an upset over a powerful Army team. Later on, as head football coach at Notre Dame, Rockne achieved great success winning three national championships and losing only 12 games in 13 years. He also capti-

Lou Holtz had plenty to smile about while at Notre Dame. His 100 victories at the Irish helm rank him second to the great Knute Rockne.

Holtz led the 1988 Fighting Irish to a 12–0 record and the school's first national championship since 1977.

vated the entire nation with his intelligence, enthusiasm, ability to motivate, and sense of humor. Unfortunately, his life was cut short when he died in a plane crash, and the entire country mourned his loss.

Frank Leahy played for Rockne and got the call to lead the Fighting Irish in 1941. He won four national championships in his 11 years as head coach, and in a four-year period, Notre Dame never lost a single football game.

After a down period, Ara Parseghian was selected as head coach of Notre Dame. As leader of the Northwestern Wildcats, his teams had beaten Notre Dame four years straight. Parseghian won two national championships in his

11-year reign with the Irish and annually had Notre Dame ranked among the best in the country.

After Ara Parseghian, Notre Dame's success continued with Dan Devine, who won a national championship in 1977 and kept Notre Dame's football teams among the very elite.

Players

No school has had more All-Americans or Heisman Trophy winners than Notre Dame. The number of athletes who've achieved greatness at Notre Dame is astounding. But what would a discussion of Notre Dame's history be without mentioning George Gipp, the Four Horsemen,

Frank Carideo, Angelo Bertelli, Creighton Miller, Johnny Lujack, Leon Hart, Paul Hornung, John Huarte, Joe Theismann, Joe Montana, Ross Browner, Vagas Ferguson, Steve Beuerlein, Tim Brown, Frank Stams, "Rocket" Ismail, Tony Rice, Ricky Watters, Jerome Bettis, Chris Zorich, Todd Lyght, Aaron Taylor, Autry Denson, Brady Quinn, and Jeff Samardzija. The list goes on and on.

Games

Notre Dame has a natural competitiveness with USC, which many consider to be the best rivalry in the country. Annually, Notre Dame's schedule is one of the most difficult in the nation and has the Irish facing off against teams such as Michigan, Michigan State, Navy, and Purdue, which typically produces some memorable games each year. Every Notre Dame fan knows about these rivalries. Before I could even ride a bike, I knew about the Notre Dame–Army game in which Knute Rockne gave his famous "Win One for The Gipper" locker-room speech, inspiring a courageous Irish comeback victory.

When I played football in grade school, our coach told us about the Notre Dame–Ohio State game in 1935. The Buckeyes led Notre Dame 13–0 at the end of the third quarter, but the Irish somehow rallied for three touchdowns to win 18–13.

But as a kid, no game was as memorable to me as the Notre Dame–Army game of 1946, which was played at Yankee Stadium. The two great teams ended in a scoreless tie, as Johnny Lujack tackled Doc Blanchard in an open field to prevent a game-winning touchdown.

I vividly recall watching on television the 1966 game in which an undefeated and No. 1-ranked Notre Dame took on No. 2 Michigan State—another hard-fought game that ended in a 10–10 tie.

To demonstrate how special Notre Dame football is to the country, when Alabama's legendary head coach Paul "Bear" Bryant retired, I called to congratulate him on his great career and for being the winningest coach of all time. I'll never forget his remark: "Thanks, Lou, but I'll be remembered as the coach that couldn't beat Notre Dame." His aspiration was to beat Notre Dame, but he never did during his entire illustrious career.

I was fortunate to coach in many games that people feel were special, but, as the coach of Notre Dame football, it's about more than just the game. It's about the total experience, and it's not complete until you kneel at the Grotto, visit Sacred Heart Basilica, attend a pep rally, sit in the stadium, see Touchdown Jesus, and listen to the band playing on the steps of the Administration Building on the morning of a game. Yes, Notre Dame football is more than just the game itself. When I think about attending the team mass on game days, marching over to the stadium encouraged by thousands of fans along the way, or touching the "Play Like A Champion Today" sign on the way to the field, it still sends chills up my spine.

Students

Nowhere do students play a more integral part of the game than at Notre Dame. They never sit during football games, and the overture to start the fourth quarter is something everyone should experience. Their enthusiasm, sincerity, and loyalty to the university are second to none, and they take that dedication with them the rest of their lives.

But Notre Dame is about more than just football. The success of the athletes and the students who leave Notre Dame wasn't achieved overnight, and it couldn't have happened without great leaders such as Father Theodore

Hesburgh and Father "Ned" Joyce, who each presided over Notre Dame for 35 years. One of my greatest thrills in life is that I was hired by these two incredible leaders and had the great fortune to receive excellent guidance from them during my 11 years as head coach. Father Hesburgh told my wife and me that the two smartest things he ever did were: 1) make Notre Dame coeducational, because it couldn't be a great university by eliminating one half of the most talented students in the world, and 2) make the Board of Trustees non-secular.

The Band

The Irish Guard brings such great enthusiasm to the contests, but often the band doesn't get the recognition it deserves for its commitment to excellence. And what song could be greater or more inspiring than the "Notre Dame Victory March"? "Cheer, cheer for old Notre Dame. Wake up the echoes cheering her name. Send a volley cheer on high. Shake down the thunder from the sky. What though the odds be great or small. Old Notre Dame will win over all. While her loyal sons are marching onward to victory."

Loyalty

Over the years, the interest in Notre Dame football grew to monstrous proportions, and in the early 1990s, NBC signed a contract to televise all of the team's home football games live. Even this did not diminish the desire to see the Fighting Irish play in person, so in the mid-1990s, Notre Dame Stadium was expanded to hold 80,000, and even still, there is great demand for tickets.

I was blessed to be at Notre Dame and even more fortunate to have three of my children attend the university. I've followed the school from afar, I've followed it as a father, and I've followed it as an insider who was overjoyed to be part of its long-standing traditions. Words cannot describe the love I have for Notre Dame, which is why my wife and I plan to be buried on the campus overlooking the old golf course and the Golden Dome.

This book is long overdue. I'm sure you'll enjoy it as much as I have because it chronicles the history, tradition, and mystique of Notre Dame football from an insider's point of view. Every Notre Dame fan has an obligation to ensure that the next generation realizes what makes Notre Dame special. This book will assure that the great efforts of so many people who have come before will prevail for years to come.

People ask me all the time what makes Notre Dame special. I reply, "If you've been there, no explanation is necessary. If you haven't been there, no explanation will satisfy you." You don't go to Notre Dame to learn how to do something; you go to Notre Dame to learn to be someone. And no school does it better than Notre Dame. There is no finer university in the world.

Lou Holtz

Holtz has been a man of many words as a football coach and analyst for ESPN. Describing the "Notre Dame mystique," however, is a task he deems impossible to those who have not experienced it for themselves.

MODEST BEGINNINGS

1887–1917

Notre Dame football did not begin with Knute Rockne. It started with a squad from the University of Michigan paying a visit to South Bend, Indiana, to teach a group of students how to play the game. The boys from Notre Dame proved to be quick learners, setting off in a direction that would shape the game for years to come.

This football was used in the second game of the 1909 season, a 60–11 Irish rout of Rose Poly-technic Institute in South Bend.

These members of the very first Notre Dame football team muddied up their white jerseys in an 8–0 loss to Michigan in November 1887.

Notre Dame lost to Michigan on back-to-back days in April 1888. The Wolverines won this game, 26–6, before earning a 10–4 triumph the following day.

The Birth and Early Days of Notre Dame Football

This program from an early Notre Dame–Michigan game included an explanation of the rules of football. Touchdowns were worth four points apiece and field goals garnered five.

A November 1869 battle between Rutgers and the College of New Jersey (now Princeton University) is widely considered to have kicked off college football in the United States. But by the late 1800s, football was not yet popular outside a handful of schools in the East, where Walter Camp, the "Father of American Football," was steering Yale to prominence. In 1879, the University of Michigan organized its first team. Eight years later, a stopover at the University of Notre Dame by Michigan's football team may have changed the course of college football more than any other contest.

George DeHaven and William Harless, two members of that Michigan team, had transferred to the university from Notre Dame. After receiving a letter from a former schoolmate, they agreed to stop on their way to a game in Chicago and teach a group of Notre Dame students the rules of the game. For good measure, they shut out their pupils by a score of 8–0 on November 23,

1887. It was a productive day, the Michigan men agreed. They added a win to their ledger, were treated to lunch and a tour of the campus, and perhaps gave themselves a new rival to push around in years to come.

"The occasion has started an enthusiastic football boom," Notre Dame's student publication, *Scholastic*, reported of the Wednesday morning game, which was contested on a muddy campus field and attended by most of the small school's students, who had been given a holiday. "And it is hoped that coming years will witness a series of these contests."

The boom that began that Wednesday has taken over fall Saturdays in South Bend in a manner that no one could have predicted. It took a while, of course, and there were years when the games seemed only important to the dozen or so young men who suited up. The Catholics—as the Notre Dame squad was called at the time—suffered two more losses to Michigan in the spring of 1888, before notching their first victory ever, a 20–0 shut out of Chicago's Harvard Prep that December. It was during the team's first road game—a 9–0 victory at Northwestern on November 14, 1889—that students on the Evanston, Illinois, campus first referred to their Catholic opponents derogatorily as the "Fighting Irish."

Notre Dame would not field another football team until 1892, but in the meantime, a movement was taking shape to raise the level of football on campus. An intramural football enthusiast named James Kivlan wrote to Camp at Yale, asking for advice on organizing a team. Camp wrote back, and

James McWeeney coached the 1899 Fighting Irish to a 6–3–1 record, surpassing the previous school mark for victories by two wins.

Floot-Ball Game.

UNIVERSITY OF MICHIGAN Vs. UNIVERSITY OF NOTRE DAME.

PLAYERS.

U. OF M.		U. N. D.
W. W. HARLESS,	*Center Rusher*	F. FEHR,
G. W. DEHAVEN,	*Rusher*	E. SAWKINS,
J. H. DUFFIE,	"	P. J. NELSON,
G. A. WOOD,	"	G. A. HOUCK,
L. MACMILLAN,	"	E. MELADY,
F. TOWNSEND,	"	J. HEPBURN,
E. M. SPRAGUE,	"	F. SPRINGER,
R. T. FARRAND,	*Quarter Back*	J. E. CUSACK,
J. H. DUFFY (Capt.),	*Half Back*	H. LUHN (Capt.),
J. E. DUFFY,	"	H. JEWETT,
E. MACFADDEN,	*Goal*	E. PRUDHOMME.

POINTS IN THE GAME.

Touch-down, 4 points; Goal kicked from touch-down, 2; Field kick over goal, 5; Safety Touch-down by side in its own goal, 2 (for their opponents).

EXPLANATION OF THE AMERICAN COLLEGE GAME OF FOOTBALL.

The grounds must be 330 ft. in length, 160 ft. in width, with a goal placed in the middle of each goal-line, composed of two upright posts 18½ ft. apart, with cross-bar 10 ft. from ground. Time of a game is one hour and a half, divided into two innings of 45 min. Between the innings there is intermission of 10 min.

Each side, while defending its own goal, necessarily faces the goal of its opponents ; and its object is to advance the ball by running with it or by kicking it towards opposing goal-line, to plant the ball on the ground on the other side of opponents' goal-line, which constitutes a "touch-down" (4 points), and to kick the ball over the cross-bar of opponents' goal, or force opponents to make a "safety" touch-down in their own territory (2 points).

When a touch-down is made, the ball is taken into the field in front of the goal where touch down was effected, and one man, lying on the ground holds the ball in a proper position ; another, when the ball is dropped, kicks it ; if the ball goes over the cross-bar it counts 2 points, in addition to the 4 points for the touch-down; and if the goal is missed it counts nothing. A goal kicked from the field without a touch-down counts 5 points, and a "safety" touch-down counts 2 points against side making it. A "safety" is made by a side its own goal to prevent opponents from scoring on a touch-down by themselves.

The goal-lines are those on which goals are erected. Touch-downs to score, can be made at back of these lines only. When the player puts the ball down on any other part of the grounds, it counts nothing. When a player holding the ball is caught, he may cry "down," and the ball is put into play again by a process known as "lining up." When the ball crosses boundary lines on side of field it is "in touch," and is put in play kicking it, throwing it, or bounding and running with it.

Kivlan took his advice, becoming a part-time coach and on-campus spokesperson for the game. Only two games were played against outside competition in 1892, but the slate grew to five games in each of the next two seasons, and James L. Morrison became the first official Notre Dame football coach in 1894. It was an unpaid position at the time.

Football was a primitive game in those days, looking more like rugby than its modern-day interpretation. "We'd bunch together and try to wedge the ball forward for the five yards needed for a first down," recalled Frank Fehr, a lineman for Notre Dame from 1887 to 1889.

> "The Michigan players really helped us with the rules and the strategy of the game. We had been playing what we called football on the campus, but we could see after the Michigan visit that we had to become more organized. The trouble was that we didn't really know much about it, just that it was a game that would be fun."
>
> —Frank Fehr, who played in Notre Dame's first organized football game in 1887

Camp's advice helped revive interscholastic play, and a campaign by *Scholastic* lobbied to keep it going. But it was the influence of another coaching legend that helped Notre Dame advance in the game. In 1894, Amos Alonzo Stagg had coached and mentored Frank E. Hering at the University of Chicago. Hering then served as player-coach at Bucknell University in central Pennsylvania before taking the same role in South Bend in 1896.

As the team's first student-coach and later its first paid boss, Hering was a groundbreaker. He added focus to Notre Dame's scheduling, preferring to play the likes of midwestern colleges such as Purdue, Michigan State, the University of Chicago, or old rival Michigan rather than taking on any high school or small college looking for a tussle. In 1897, Stagg allegedly brought in nonstudent "ringers" to ensure a 34–5 victory over his former student.

Hering also served as a de facto athletic director in the late 1890s, and it was under his watch that the university and its president Andrew Morrissey imposed rules that required all players to be Notre Dame students, maintain amateur status, and put schoolwork first. Any student earning grades of less than 75 percent would not be allowed to compete.

Hering's coaching record was 12–6–1 over three seasons, but Michigan handed his last Notre Dame team a 23–0 setback in October 1898. Coach James McWeeney and the 1899 team fared slightly better against the Wolverines, falling 12–0. But when helmetless push came to rugby-style shove, the Fighting Irish closed the 19th century indebted to their rivals from the Great Lakes State.

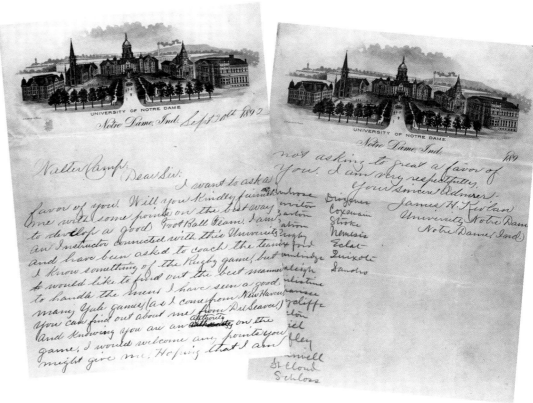

In this 1892 letter to Yale coach Walter Camp, Notre Dame instructor James Kivlan asked for advice on organizing a football team, which helped elevate the fledgling sport on the South Bend campus.

"Cheer, Cheer for Old Notre Dame"

Perhaps you don't know what a "volley cheer" is, but if you're a Fighting Irish fan, chances are you've sung those words (or at least hummed them) before, during, or after a Notre Dame game.

Voted "the greatest of all fight songs" at college football's 1969 centennial celebration, the "Notre Dame Victory March" was written more than 100 years ago by the Shea brothers, Notre Dame alumni who noticed that the Fighting Irish lacked an official song. Michael Shea, a 1905 Notre Dame graduate and a priest in Ossining, New York, wrote the music on a piano. His brother John, who completed Notre Dame degrees in 1906 and 1908 and later became a Massachusetts state senator, penned the words.

Though the university had a marching band some 60 years before the song was copyrighted in 1908, the "Notre Dame Victory March" was first performed not on a football field but in a Holyoke, Massachusetts, church, where Michael Shea played it on the organ as parishioners hummed along easily. Its Notre Dame debut came the following year when it was performed in the rotunda of the Administration Building on Easter Sunday 1909. The Shea brothers gladly presented it to their alma mater as a gift.

It's a gift that's been giving to fans of Notre Dame athletics since 1919, when it began to gain popularity on campus and was first played at a school sporting event. Since then, it has served as a goosebump-inducing soundtrack for Fighting Irish success.

The "Notre Dame Victory March" had not yet been written at the time of this 1906 photo, but the school's marching band still kept fans tapping their toes.

Rally sons of Notre Dame:
Sing her glory and sound her fame,
Raise her Gold and Blue
And cheer with voices true:
Rah, rah, for Notre Dame
We will fight in ev'ry game,
Strong of heart and true to her name
We will ne'er forget her
And will cheer her ever
Loyal to Notre Dame
Cheer, cheer for old Notre Dame,
Wake up the echoes cheering her name,
Send a volley cheer on high,
Shake down the thunder from the sky.
What though the odds be great or small
Old Notre Dame will win over all,
While her loyal sons are marching
Onward to victory.

This sheet music for the "Notre Dame Victory March" indicates that the song is fit for a Fighting Irish baseball team. Fans of the blue and gold in every sport know the tune—and words—by heart.

Game Day

The Nieuwland Science Center now sits on the ground where Notre Dame first staged a varsity football game—an 8–0 loss to Michigan on November 23, 1887. Needless to say, there would be many happy professors if their pupils' enthusiasm about science matched the vigor with which students embraced that opening contest.

The Notre Dame band was on hand, as was a group of cheerleaders, and nearly the entire student body gathered around a muddy pitch to witness the game and offer support for the home team.

Essentially, that sounds much like a modern Notre Dame football game. Except there were no bleachers on which to sit, no television cameras, no scoreboard, no female students (women were not admitted as undergraduates until 1972), no media—other than the school publication *Scholastic*—and the first game was played in mid-morning, due to the schedule of the train that brought Michigan's players.

Admission to this historical contest: priceless. Literally. Students and anyone else with an interest or curiosity could simply walk up and watch in the early days of Notre Dame football.

But game days changed drastically with the opening of Cartier Field in the 1890s. Warren A. Cartier, a wealthy 1887 graduate, bought the land and materials and paid for construction of the school's first enclosed stadium, built on the southern outskirts of campus. The complex also included a baseball diamond and a banked quarter-mile track for bicycle races, which were popular at the time.

By the turn of the century, students and townspeople alike had decided that watching the Notre Dame eleven was worth the price of admission, particularly because that fee could be measured in cents. Students were still admitted free of charge, so it was not unusual for a few thousand patrons to gather at Cartier Field to watch the Irish play.

Before a 1901 game against visiting Indiana University that would decide what newspapers were calling the "state championship," the *South Bend Tribune* reported that "rooter preparations are on a strong scale. Every student will be there whether he likes it or not and take part in organized cheering."

Fans—particularly Catholic ones—across the country soon began hearing about and rooting for a small school in South Bend, Indiana, that seemed willing to take on all comers, no matter the venue.

Notre Dame's first-ever homecoming game attracted 12,000 fans to Cartier Field to witness the Fighting Irish shut out Purdue 28–0 on November 6, 1920.

Fans rooting for Notre Dame in the early 1900s were on board with a winner. The Fighting Irish shut out six of the eight opponents on their 1909 schedule.

Turn-of-the-Century Football

James Faragher was a powerful tackle for Notre Dame's turn-of-the-century football team before coaching the 1902 and '03 squads.

Beating Michigan for the first time gave the 1909 Fighting Irish a special distinction at their end-of-the-year banquet. They were, indeed, "Champions of the West."

Football was evolving rapidly as the 20th century arrived. Kicking became an important part of the game, and Notre Dame had just the man to lead it into this new era. Pat O'Dea, who was legendary for his successful dropkicks of 60-plus yards during his career at the University of Wisconsin, took over as Fighting Irish coach in 1900 and led the team to a 14–4–2 record in two seasons at the helm.

In 1903, James Faragher, O'Dea's successor, coached the most dominant team in Notre Dame history. The national championship squads of Knute Rockne, Frank Leahy, and Ara Parseghian had nothing on this group. The 1903 Irish outscored their opponents by a staggering 292–0 margin, winning eight games and settling for a controversial scoreless tie against Northwestern.

"We should have won that one," said Louis "Red" Salmon, who became Notre Dame's first football All-American. "On a run for a touchdown, the official ruled that I stepped out of bounds, but I wasn't within three yards of the boundary at any time."

Just as Notre Dame was well-equipped when kicking the football came into vogue, the Fighting Irish made great use of the forward pass not long after it became legal in 1906. If passing was not an integral part of the offense under Coach Thomas Barry (12–1–1) in 1906 and 1907, it almost certainly was in Vic Place's attack in 1908, when the Irish went 8–1.

In the four seasons from 1909 to 1912, Notre Dame went undefeated three times. However, it was the 7–0–1 team of 1909 that stood out for its milestone accomplishment—beating Michigan. The Wolverines had won eight straight meetings by a combined score of 121–16 since teaching Notre Dame how to play football back in 1887.

With Harry "Red" Miller providing the bulk of the offense and Pete Vaughan and Billy Ryan finding the end zone, the Fighting Irish earned an 11–3 triumph in Ann Arbor, gaining acclaim as the "Best in the West."

Is There a Doctor in the House?

Actually, there were at least 11 young men on their way to becoming physicians when Notre Dame faced off against American Medical on October 28, 1905, in what became one of the most lopsided contests in history.

One week before American Medical visited Notre Dame, the Fighting Irish lost to Wabash in what would be their last setback on Cartier Field for more than 23 years.

From the start, the doctors found themselves in the wrong place at the wrong time. Notre Dame scored 121 points in the 25-minute first half. The second half was stopped after eight minutes to allow the visitors time for lunch between the 142–0 drubbing and their return trip to Chicago.

Believe it or not, it could have been much worse. Notre Dame missed extra-point kicks after 20 of its 27 touchdowns.

The 1905 Fighting Irish finished just one game over .500 but had the distinction of serving up a school-record 142–0 blowout of American Medical.

Early Stars: Gus, Rock, and the "Reds"

Today, Cedar Point Amusement Park in Sandusky, Ohio, is known for some of the world's most thrilling roller coasters. But during the summer of 1913, it was the birthplace of some of the most amazing plays in early college football history.

The forward pass had been in use for several years, although most of the nation's powerhouse teams still preferred the straight-ahead, run-oriented style of play. But during a summer in which they both took restaurant jobs at Cedar Point, Notre Dame roommates Knute Rockne and Gus Dorais decided to try a different route, cooking up several passing plays that would turn their opponents upside down.

With a strong right arm that belied his 5′7″, 145-pound stature, Dorais was a star pitcher for the Fighting Irish baseball team. On the football field, he experimented with a more modern way of gripping the pigskin than the open-palm approach favored by most quarterbacks of his day.

Rockne, a science whiz who planned to teach chemistry after graduating, put his sharp mind to work designing timing routes that would not require receivers such as himself to stand waiting for the ball. Instead, passes would be caught in full stride.

That fall, the roommates put their plays in motion and passed, ran, and caught their way to All-American honors, along with powerful fullback Ray Eichenlaub, during a 7–0 season. It marked the first time three Notre Dame players earned All-American accolades in the same year. In fact, only two previous Fighting Irish players had been named All-Americans. Both were nicknamed "Red" for their hair color.

Louis "Red" Salmon was Notre Dame's first big-name star. Debuting in 1900, the Syracuse, New York, native teamed with John Farley to give the team a dominant running attack. By the time he took over as captain in 1902, "Red" *was* Notre Dame football. The fullback plowed over defenders with abandon. In 1903, his dominant senior season, Salmon earned distinction as the first Fighting Irish All-American while the team compiled a 292–0 scoring margin over its helpless foes.

As if one All-American "Red" was not enough for opponents, another arrived in 1906. Harry "Red" Miller returned the first kickoff of his freshman year past midfield and rarely stopped running thereafter. In 1909—his All-American season—he led the Irish to their first victory over Michigan and kept serving Notre Dame after his graduation, as father of 1940s stars Tom and Creighton Miller.

> **"I went out for the track team, made the team, made my varsity letter. Now I had some prestige— enough to warrant another tryout for the football team."**
>
> —**Knute Rockne, on his failed initial attempt to make the Notre Dame varsity**

As a determined and dedicated player, Knute Rockne played much bigger than his size as Notre Dame's starting left end from 1911 to 1913.

Louis "Red" Salmon became Notre Dame's first All-American on a 1903 team that outscored its opponents 292–0.

Some members of the Notre Dame faculty were disappointed when Knute Rockne (front row, second from left) left his position as assistant chemistry professor to coach football full-time.

Notre Dame's Biggest Game

The most important football game in Notre Dame history was almost never played. Every season for two decades—generally in late October or early November—Army clashed with Yale. However, as the boys from West Point looked over their 1913 schedule, they noticed two things: Yale was not on the slate, and no game was scheduled for November 1.

Yale had given Lehigh that date in 1913, and Army coach Lt. Charlie Daly found every eastern football power booked when he tried to schedule another opponent. Most eastern football fans had never heard of Notre Dame. And if not for Fighting Irish coach Jesse Harper's ability to coax $1,000 in travel money from Army ($600 more than the original offer), they might not have seen the midwesterners at all.

Perhaps jittery about playing a heavily favored Army team for the first time or leg-weary from their long train ride, the Fighting Irish fumbled away two of their first three possessions. But once Notre Dame got going, the easterners were amazed at the ease with which the visitors completed downfield passes, including a 25-yarder from strong-armed quarterback Gus Dorais to Knute Rockne that kicked off the scoring.

The Cadets answered with two touchdowns for a 13–7 lead, but Rockne knew the Fighting Irish could weather the storm. "Army was just too big and too strong," he said of the Cadets's ability to stop the run. "So we decided we'd hit them with our air attack. We didn't think Army was quick enough or smart enough to adjust its defenses."

The Fighting Irish passed the Cadets silly thereafter. Dorais, whom *The New York Times* called "as agile as a cat and as restless as a jumping-jack," steered Notre Dame to the lead just before halftime. The Irish packed on three unanswered touchdowns in the fourth quarter and flew to a 35–13 rout. Dorais completed 14 of 17 passes for 243 yards, and his 40-yard pass to Rockne was the longest ever completed to that day.

Reported the *Times*, "The Notre Dame eleven swept the Army off its feet on the plains. . . . The Westerners flashed the most sensational football that has been seen in the East this year."

Less than 5,000 fans witnessed the game that marked Notre Dame's arrival as a national power.

Spectators mingled between halves of Notre Dame's 35–13 win over Army at West Point in 1913.

This expense report for Notre Dame's 1913 trip to West Point shows—among other things—that Notre Dame earned a $1,000 guarantee from Army and paid one buck for shoe repair.

Jesse Harper: Upon This "Rock" I Build . . . Notre Dame Football

Jesse Harper could serve as Exhibit A for anyone making a case that surrounding oneself with great people is the surest way to success. A native of Paw Paw, Illinois, Harper played for Amos Alonzo Stagg at the University of Chicago and then was instrumental in Knute Rockne's growth as a player and coach at Notre Dame.

Under Stagg, Harper helped the Maroons to a 1905 national championship and caught the coaching bug in the process. His first stops after graduation were Alma College in Michigan where he posted a 10–4–4 record (1906–07) and Wabash College in Indiana where he went 15–9–2 (1909–12).

But Harper's greatest accomplishment before leading Notre Dame to a 1913 upset of Army may actually have been a *loss* against the Fighting Irish. His outmanned 1911 Wabash team made a terrific upset bid before falling by a 6–3 score. Harper's work with that squad clearly impressed Notre Dame's administration, which hired him as head football coach and director of athletics in 1913. Harper was a fan of the forward pass,

Jesse Harper popularized the forward pass in South Bend, using it to run up a 34–5–1 record over five seasons as Notre Dame's head coach.

which, although legalized in 1906, was still minimally used. But when he saw some of the downfield passing plays Dorais and Rockne had practiced during the summer of 1913, the new Notre Dame boss made a decision that would stamp himself and his team as college football innovators.

Harper passed the opposition into submission. No one could keep up with the Fighting Irish. His 1913 club went 7–0, outscoring its opponents by a 268–41 margin, highlighted by the 35–13 win at Army. Notre Dame won its second game of 1914 by a 103–0 count against Rose Polytechnic Institute (now Rose–Hulman Institute of Technology) of Terre Haute, Indiana. In five years at the helm, Harper went 34–5–1.

Perhaps Harper's greatest coaching move after Rockne's 1913 graduation was hiring his former captain as an assistant. When they put their heads together, mixing the backfield shift Harper learned from Stagg with Rockne's suggestion to put both ends on the move, the result was the "Notre Dame shift"—a shuffle that confounded defenses for years.

But an even greater shift was coming. "When I resigned in 1918," Harper said, "I insisted that Rockne should be given the job, and for weeks I argued with Father [school president John W.] Cavanaugh that 'Rock' could do a better job than anyone else."

How could Father Cavanaugh refuse? After all, "Rock" had learned from a great one himself. A dominant era of Notre Dame football had begun.

Gus Dorais enjoyed 70 years as the only four-year starting quarterback in Notre Dame history—until Blair Kiel came along in 1980. He was also Notre Dame's first consensus All-American.

ARMY ATHLETIC COUNCIL
UNITED STATES MILITARY ACADEMY
WEST POINT, NEW YORK

AGREEMENT.

FOR THE SEASON OF 1913 BETWEEN THE *University of Notre Dame*
Athletic Association and the ARMY ATHLETIC COUNCIL.

Article 1.- The date of the game between the two teams shall be
November first, at West Point, N. Y.

Article 11.- The visiting team shall receive at West Point a
guarantee of *One thousand* dollars ($ *1000 .00*).

Article 111.- The home team agrees to furnish grounds and stands
necessary, and to supply police and officials.

Article 1V.- It is further understood that this agreement in no-
wise establishes a precedent which shall in any way influence the
games of any subsequent year.

Manager, *Notre Dame Football Team.*

Manager, Army Football Team.

(Approved)

1st Lieut., Corps of Engineers,
Army Football Representative.

One of Jesse Harper's duties in 1913, during his first year as Fighting Irish head coach, was signing this agreement for a game against Army at West Point. Notre Dame won 35–13.

Notre Dame's 1910 football team went 4–1–1 and made it onto the cover of a 1911 calendar fit for an avid Fighting Irish fan.

Snow Scene at Notre Dame, Ind.

Father Edward Sorin founded the University of Notre Dame in 1842— some 45 years before the school embraced football.

This early 20th-century postcard depicts a typical winter day on the Notre Dame campus.

Notre Dame uniforms of the 1800s were anything but uniform. Not until 1914 did the Irish begin wearing numbers on their jerseys.

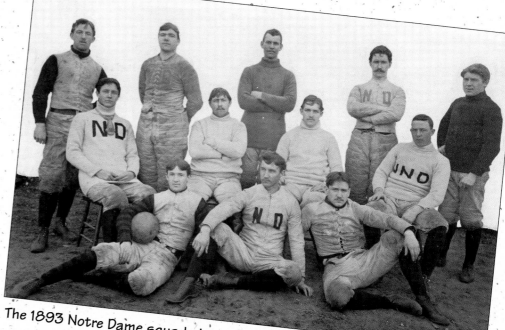

The 1893 Notre Dame squad played five games—two more than any previous Fighting Irish club—winning the first four before a New Year's Day 1894 loss to the University of Chicago.

By finally beating Michigan during an undefeated 1909 season, Notre Dame earned its claim to the title "Champions of the West."

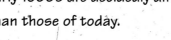

These leather shoulder pads from the early 1900s are decidedly different than those of today.

ROCK, THE GIPPER, AND THE FOUR HORSEMEN

1918–1940

Between World Wars I and II, Notre Dame gave college football some of its most lasting nicknames. The Fighting Irish also captured their first national championships, emerging as the nation's most dominant and widely followed program led by perhaps the greatest coach of all time.

Fighting Irish pennants have changed through the years, but the blue and gold of Notre Dame have not.

A November 21, 1931, game against Southern Cal attracted the first capacity crowd at Notre Dame Stadium—50,731 patrons. The Trojans prevailed 16–14.

The Golden Dome looms large in the distance during a spirited Fighting Irish football practice in the 1920s.

COACHING

KNUTE ROCKNE

The FOUR WINNERS

by

KNUTE ROCKNE

The FOUR WINNERS

the Head
the Hands
the Foot
the Ball

by

KNUTE ROCKNE

Knute Rockne was more than a great football coach. He was also a renowned public speaker, wrote a regular newspaper column, and authored books on coaching and football fundamentals.

No one did more for Notre Dame football—and perhaps football in general—than the beloved Knute Rockne.

Knute Rockne:
Setting the Standard

The Irish were down. The breaks were beating the boys. Instead of turning to one of his legendary speeches, Knute Rockne let his players stew over a 10–0 halftime deficit against Northwestern. They sat, heads in their hands or staring toward the door, waiting for their coach to chew up their poor first-half effort in the 1925 game. After all, Notre Dame looked well on its way to losing on Cartier Field for the first time in 20 years.

They waited. Finally, in walked a seething Coach Rockne. "The Fighting Irish," the coach said in a dismissive tone, as tackle Joe Boland would later recall. "Well, you'll be able to tell your grandchildren you're the first Notre Dame team that ever quit."

Rockne then told Assistant Coach Hunk Anderson to take over, adding that he was "through with 'em." He walked out. Stunned players looked at one another, charged through the door, and hammered the Northwestern defense for long touchdown drives on their first two possessions of the second half. Rockne returned to the sideline sometime before his troops put the finishing touches on a 13–10 victory.

To this day, coaches call inspirational locker-room talks "Knute Rockne speeches." They look for ways to coax teams to "win one for The Gipper." While it's true that Rockne could motivate players like no one

else, this was just one aspect of his brilliance as coach, leader, and man.

The son of a carriage maker, Knute Rockne was born in Norway and moved to Chicago with his family at age five. After high school, he worked as a post office dispatcher for four years, saving enough money to enroll at Notre Dame at age 22. As a varsity end, Rockne and quarterback Gus Dorais developed downfield passing plays that helped Notre Dame become the talk of college football. Mean-

Not one to oversee practices from a tower, Rockne could often be found on the field demonstrating proper technique to his players.

Official—

FOOTBALL
SCHEDULE

Notre Dame University

1914

JESSE HARPER
Coach

K. ROCKNE
Ass't Coach

KEITH K. "DEAK" JONES
Captain

JERRY McCARTHY
Secretary

Knute Rockne served as an assistant coach under Jesse Harper, whose teams posted a 34–5–1 record in five seasons from 1913 to 1917.

"One man practicing sportsmanship is far better than 50 preaching it."

—Knute Rockne

while, his work in the classroom had university priests and administrators convinced they were producing an outstanding chemistry professor. Instead, they produced a man whose gifts crossed the spectrum.

There was Rockne the actor. He once had an Army defensive back believing he was hobbled before racing past him for a 40-yard reception, the longest ever at the time. As a coach, he became known for not letting the facts stand in the way of an emotional speech.

There was Rockne the psychologist. Whether speaking to players, businesspeople, or a classroom—he took a job as an assistant chemistry professor at Notre Dame on the condition that he could help coach football— Rockne had an understanding of the human psyche that allowed him to deliver the right message in the right manner.

There was Rockne the innovator. He did not invent the forward pass or the offensive motion that some called the

Top: *Rockne addresses his team at Cartier Field on September 15, 1930, just three weeks before the Fighting Irish opened what would be his final season with a 20–14 victory over SMU.*

Early-season practices in South Bend could warm up pretty quickly, especially if a player wasn't executing to Rockne's satisfaction.

"Rockne shift." He did, however, bring his unique vision to those and other offensive tactics, coaching the game in a way that pioneers like Camp, Yost, Stagg, and Warner before him had never imagined.

And there was Rockne the leader. As charismatic as any politician, Rockne took Notre Dame football to new heights. His record of 105 wins, 12 losses, and 5 ties set a standard for winning percentage that no Division I coach has equaled. Five of his teams went undefeated and untied. Just as important, his relentless demand for perfection shaped his team's personality, helping the Fighting Irish gain a national following.

"No one who knew Rock closely could ever forget him," penned legendary sportswriter Grantland Rice. "In addition to his skill and all-around ability as a football coach, he had a certain indescribable flame—a physical and mental vitality that few men have possessed."

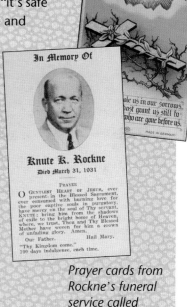

Buttons such as this one honored Rockne and the impact he made on and off the field.

Knute Rockne and his wife, Bonnie, share a smile.

The Loss of a Legend

In early March 1931, Knute Rockne was asked by *New York Times* reporter John Kieran his opinion on flying.

"With a good pilot and a good plane," the Notre Dame coach said, "it's safe and it saves you a lot of time and discomfort."

Three weeks later, while traveling from Miami to Los Angeles to assist in the film production of *The Spirit of Notre Dame*, Rockne had stopped to visit his two sons in Kansas City, Missouri. On March 31, 1931, he and seven others boarded TWA flight 599. All eight were killed when the plane lost a wing and plummeted into a field near Bazaar, Kansas.

Some 1,400 mourners filled Sacred Heart Basilica for Rockne's funeral mass. Millions more listened on the radio.

Thousands paid their respects outside Notre Dame's Sacred Heart Basilica while 1,400 friends and family members mourned inside. Millions listened to the national radio broadcast, hearing Father Charles L. O'Donnell, Notre Dame's president, eulogize: "In an age that has stamped itself as the era of the 'go-getter'... he was a 'go-giver.'"

Prayer cards from Rockne's funeral service called for "a crown of unfading glory."

Rockne's death and burial were not only front-page news in South Bend but in newspapers all over the country. To so many people in so many places, he was more than just a football coach.

Knute Rockne's death in 1931 was front-page news around the world, but nowhere did it break more hearts than on a small college campus in South Bend, Indiana.

The Notre Dame Scholastic

Extra   Extra

Disce-Quasi-Semper-Victurus~Vive-Quasi-Cras-Moriturus

MARCH 31, 1931.

COACH K. K. ROCKNE KILLED

Famed Notre Dame Mentor Dies In Crash Near Emporia, Kansas

Knute K. Rockne, fourteen years coach at Notre Dame, was killed this noon in an airplane crash near Emporia, Kansas. Mr. Rockne was enroute to Los Angeles, where he was scheduled to deliver an address.

There were four other persons in the plane besides Mr. Rockne. All were killed.

Confirmation of the accident was received from the Associated Press, following radio reports that the accident had occurred. Official confirmation was received shortly before one o'clock.

Telegrams and phone calls besieged the Rockne household as the news reached South Bend. Mrs. Rockne, who is on a vacation with the two sons in Florida, could not be reached.

The plane, a Transcontinental and Western air passenger and air mail plane, crashed in flames in a pasture several miles southwest of Bazaar, Kansas.

The air liner landed on a farm owned by Seward Baker, who reported the accident immediately to authorities. Local officials were not able to identify the victims immediately.

The crash was seen by Edward Baker, a farm youth, who was feeding cattle nearby. His statement is that something in the craft exploded. A short time later it nosed into the earth. Ambulances were sent from Cottonwood Falls.

"Hunk" Anderson and Jack Chevigny, assistant coaches, will head a delegation to go to Kansas City. The party is to leave immediately.

Campus Stirred by News of Knute Rockne's Tragic Death

As the news reached the Notre Dame campus that Knute Rockne had been tragically killed in an airplane crash, excited, bare-headed students gathered in small groups discussing in low tones the first reports of the accident.

Excitement ran rampant. Telephones in all of the halls were used to get in touch with local newspapers. The publications office was besieged with a hundred requests for official confirmation. Hall chapels were crowded with students, while in some parts of the campus organized prayer was conducted.

The air hung heavy with expectancy. The student body was hoping against hope that the rumor would prove false,

(Continued on Page 4)

BULLETIN

(By Associated Press.)

Emporia, Kansas. — Knute Rockne boarded an airplane enroute to California at 9:15 o'clock this morning. At about 11:00 A.M. the ship, identified by its department of commerce license number, crashed and burned as it fought a fog and storm enroute to Wichita, Kan.

The body of Rockne and the other victims had not been definitely identified at the scene, but it was certain that the noted coach was a passenger on the merchant liner. All those aboard her were killed.

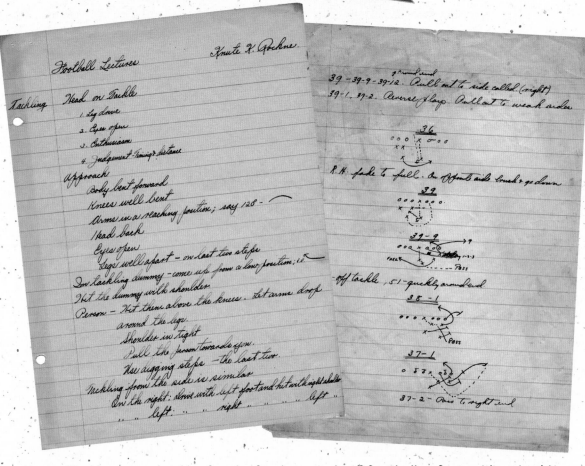

Knute Rockne was a stickler for the fundamentals of football, a fact evident in this well-scripted lecture on sound tackling. Fakes, reverses, and pass plays were all in Rockne's football playbook. In this case, they all appeared on one notebook page.

This bio of Knute Rockne, taken from his 1914 yearbook, praises his sense of humor, chemistry prowess, and pole-vaulting ability in addition to his football skills. It also points out rather prophetically that he is "made of the stuff that spells success."

KNUTE KENNITH ROCKNE, B. S. in Chem.

If "Rock" had done nothing else than captain the 1913 eleven of Notre Dame, his fame would be assured. But he has made other bids for renown. Do not think, expectant reader, that we can name them all. We can not omit, however, to tell that he was unanimous choice last fall for all-Western end; that he pole-vaulted twelve-feet-three at Evanston this spring. We fain would attest that he blows a whistle in the orchestra, was captain of our Junior crew, was star commedienne on the local stage and Editor of the "Dome." Among others, he was a maid of the queen of the Fall Festival, and subsequently, the occasion for a forty-foot petition. Knute is a first rate chemist, even though he used to associate with Jonny Plant in North Division High in Chicago, and is made of the stuff that spells success.

Gerry Miller, who played for the Fighting Irish from 1922 to 1924, lounges on the beach in Sandusky, Ohio, with the man who coached several members of his family, including his brother Don of Four Horsemen fame.

A young Rockne (right) showed a keen interest in sports besides football, so perhaps it was Notre Dame's good fortune that he did not pursue a career as a Wimbledon hopeful.

Contract of Employment

THIS AGREEMENT, made on the 25th day of March A.D. 19 24 by and between Knute K. Rockne, of South Bend, State of Indiana party of the first part, and the Reverend Matthew Walsh, C. S. C., President of the University of Notre Dame Du Lac, a corporation created and existing by and under the laws of the State of Indiana, with its chief seat at Notre Dame, St. Joseph County, in said State, party of the second part, Witnesseth, That the said party of the first part promises and agrees hereby faithfully, diligently and obediently, as required by the nature of his employment, to work for and serve the said party of the second part and his authorized representatives in the capacity or position of instructor in said University, for the period of one academic year of ten months, commencing on the first day of September, A. D. 1924, and ending on the 30th day of the succeeding June, 1934, for the sum total of 10,000 annual salary dollars, which may be received, if desired, in monthly installments as earned.

It is likewise understood and agreed by and between the parties hereto, that the said party of the first part shall faithfully and diligently, prudently and creditably, perform the duties devolving upon him; that while his bearing toward students and associates shall be manly and dignified, straightforward and honorable, it must at the same time be marked by gentlemanly courtesy and an obliging disposition, so as to afford in itself, if possible, a wholesome lesson to the young; that he shall vigilantly guard against becoming a cause of reproach or scandal at Notre Dame or elsewhere by indulgence in the use of intoxicating liquors or the commission otherwise of acts discreditable and reprehensible, and that he shall so conduct himself as to serve honorably in the domain of Catholic education, and do nothing to jeopard the confidence and good will of the patrons and friends of said University. And it is further understood and agreed by and between the parties hereto that if the said party of the first part should violate any of the terms of this agreement, or so demean himself as to render impracticable his continuance in the employment of said University, as where he menaces its good name or reputation for efficiency in educational work, or where he allows anger and passion to dominate his reason to the extent of striking or having personal encounters with students, it shall be the unquestioned right of the said party of the second part to dispense with and end his term of employment as by discharge, to which the said party of the first part specifically agrees, waiving all further rights under this contract, on giving him one month's notice and paying the stated salary pro rata to the end of such month, and for no other month or portion of said academic year, thus terminating this agreement as completely to all intents and purposes as though it had never existed.

And it is likewise understood and agreed by and between the parties hereto that the death or long-continued and disabling sickness of the said party of the first part shall likewise terminate this agreement, and all further claims for salary under it at the election of said party of the second part on giving a month's notice and paying the prescribed salary pro rata to the end of that time.

By mutual consent of the parties hereto, this agreement may be renewed from year to year, or it may be modified to meet altered conditions by a change of its terms or the insertion of additional provisions.

IN WITNESS WHEREOF, the said parties have hereunto set their hands at Notre Dame, in said County and State, the day and year first above mentioned.

[Signed] Knute K Rockne

[Signed] Matthew J Walsh c. s. c.

Knute Rockne's 1924 Notre Dame football contract called for him to be paid $10,000 annually over a ten-year period.

Using arrows and dotted lines vaguely resembling some of his football plays, Rockne took notes for what appears to be a botany lesson at Notre Dame.

Time magazine featured Rockne on the cover of a 1927 issue. Days later, the Fighting Irish saw their unbeaten season foiled by an 18–0 loss to Army, but they rebounded to finish 7–1–1.

Studebaker automobiles, which were made in South Bend, honored Notre Dame's late football coach with a Rockne model in 1932. The '33 model was advertised in The New Yorker.

Rockne was *made to order* for New York!

ROCKNE $585
Sponsored and Guaranteed by Studebaker

Grace and Glory on the Gridiron: The Legendary George Gipp

Knute Rockne knew that George Gipp was not a saint. Notre Dame's coach was aware that his affable star player enjoyed hustling pool in South Bend halls for money, carousing with the late-night crowd, and trying to impress the ladies. Gipp was known to gamble on sporting events, once betting that he would score more points himself than Army would manage as a team in a 1920 game against the Fighting Irish. His professors would have preferred the same ambition in the classroom, but class work did not hold Gipp's interest much.

Rockne was not blind to Gipp's hard-living style off the field, but the coach also held the Laurium, Michigan, native in high regard for his ability to deliver time and again. Gipp was a baseball prodigy who once hit .494 for his hometown team and crushed the longest home run ever hit in its ballpark. At age 21, he arrived at Notre Dame on a baseball scholarship.

Gipp did not play organized football in high school, and with his slight build (6'0", 175 pounds), dreams of lettering in two sports in South Bend were far from his mind. That is, until Rockne—then an assistant coach under Jesse Harper—watched him drop-kick a ball some 60 yards in a perfect spiral.

"Why aren't you out for the freshman squad?" Rockne asked.

"Football isn't my game," replied Gipp.

That changed quickly. While he kept playing baseball—some reports say he even played "town ball" for money

Just days before his untimely death, George Gipp (bottom row, right) was named to the Walter Camp All-America Team after leading the Irish in rushing, passing, kickoff return yardage, and scoring in 1920.

Nicknamed "The Gipper," George Gipp was a driving force behind Notre Dame's success between 1917 and 1920. He set a school career rushing record that lasted more than 50 years.

under an alias while at Notre Dame—Gipp was persuaded by Rockne to give football a try. That year, in a freshman game, he drop-kicked a ball through the uprights from 62 yards away. He quickly became "The Gipper," the best all-around weapon the Fighting Irish varsity had in its arsenal.

The halfback led Notre Dame in rushing and passing in each of his three full varsity seasons, beginning in 1918. Those were also Rockne's first three years as head coach, contributing to the tight bond between the two. Gipp's 2,341 career rushing yards stood as a school record for 58 years until broken by Jerome Heavens in 1978. His raw speed, elusive moves, accurate arm, and jaw-dropping

"One for The Gipper"

The only two people who knew what was said in George Gipp's hospital room in the days before his 1920 death were Gipp himself and Knute Rockne. The latter was a coach not above stretching the truth in the name of a good pep talk.

We do know this: Eight years later, as Notre Dame faced an undefeated Army powerhouse, "Rock" gave his account in the most famous locker-room speech in football history.

"None of you ever knew George Gipp," he said. "It was long before your time. But you know what a tradition he is at Notre Dame. . . .

Ronald Reagan portrayed a dying George Gipp in Knute Rockne All American.

"The last thing he said to me, 'Rock,' he said, 'sometime, when the team is up against it, and the breaks are beating the boys, tell them to go out there with all they got and win just one for The Gipper. . . . I don't know where I'll be then, Rock, but I'll know about it, and I'll be happy.'"

The final score: Notre Dame 12, Army 6. One for The Gipper.

GEO. GIPP
1895–1920

kicks led Rockne's 1919 and 1920 teams to matching 9–0–0 records as Notre Dame became a household name among college football fans.

With Gipp, however, life was never routine. He was dismissed from school before the 1920 season for missing too many classes. Rockne pleaded with administrators and arranged an oral exam in which Gipp would have to prove his mettle before a group of law professors. Two hours later, he emerged with a high score and a nonchalant assessment: "Made it."

During that year—the last of his football career and his life—he was spectacular. In a 27–17 win against Army, Gipp rushed for 150 yards, passed for 123 yards and a touchdown, returned two punts for 50 yards, kicked brilliantly, and added three extra points. Bill Corum of the *New York Journal American* wrote: "Many Notre Dame stars have climbed the glory ladder of raw courage to greatness, but none further than George Gipp on this single day. . . . It was a show of immortality."

Of course, it was not long before Gipp's mortality made headlines, too. Three weeks later, he developed strep throat that turned into pneumonia. Some say it was brought on by sleeping on the cold steps outside Washington Hall on a night when he broke curfew. Others attribute it to cold-weather punting lessons he provided to students.

As Gipp battled for his life at St. Joseph's Hospital, he converted to Catholicism, learned he had been named an All-American by *Collier's Magazine,* and was signed by the Chicago Cubs. He died December 14, 1920, at age 25.

> **"Gipp was one of the greatest. His kind comes once in every generation."**
>
> **—Knute Rockne**

"The Gipper" impressed Rockne with his booming kicks during his early practices at Notre Dame.

GIPP'S DEATH GRIEVES GRID FAND[O]

STUDENT BODY PLANS ITS FINAL TRIBUTE TO IDOL

Team Mates to Accompany Body to Calumet Thursday—Flags at Half Mast —Dies on Day He is Honored as Greatest Fullback.

With American football fandom grieving today over the death of George Gipp, arrangements were being completed at Notre Dame university for the entire student body to pay final tribute to its idol of the gridiron.

While messages of sympathy were pouring in from football men throughout the nation, news was received that Gipp's death apparently took place just as he was reaching the height of his career. Announcement was made by Walter Camp, America's football authority, that the Notre Dame star is his selection as the greatest fullback of the year.

Hearts Heavy.

Notre Dame students accept Fate's grim decision with heavy hearts already prepared for the shock. Flags on the Notre Dame campus and on the South Bend court house were at half mast throughout Monday forenoon. Outwardly the school goes on in a normal manner; but the silence is only a reaction from the constant vigilies, prayers, hope and despair during the period of Gipp's illness. The university's part in the funeral services which will follow the wishes of the family of the dead boy.

Plan Procession.

Walter Larson, Hartley Anderson and Percy Wilcox, fellow townsmen and Percy Wilcox, who have been his companions at high school and college, will make their last journey with players of the football squad probably will accompany the body to Calumet, Mich., and if tentative plans are followed the entire student body will march in procession from the McCann undertaking parlors to the L. T. C. station Wednesday morn.

The funeral party, including the bereaved mother, sister and brother and the delegation of teammates leave South Bend at 10:25 ... Chicago

GIPP'S DEATH IS SHOCK TO FANDOM

(CONTINUED FROM PAGE ONE)

ability was surpassed by a gritty featured all his work on the iron, and was the marvel of attending physicians. The inspiring feature of his character was his deep affection for his mother whom in his death I feel loss."

Frank Coughlin, leader of football team which Gipp shot to fame, and who is arranging the student action in the services, gave the following statement:

"George Gipp was perhaps the greatest athlete I have ever known. He was a man among men, brilliant and unassuming; and has endeared himself to the heart of every Notre Dame student by his athletic prowess, magnetic personality, keen mind and his keen love for the old school. He will forever be remembered as a friend, a student, an athlete and a gentleman to know him was to love him."

Not Due to Injury.

Attending physicians state that Gipp's death was in no sense the result of a football injury but the open air training of the athletic field benefited rather than injured his health. He was a victim of throat trouble.

All sports have been discontinued at Notre Dame during the period of the funeral services. The basket ball games with Purdue and the Em-Boes of Indianapolis have been cancelled, out of respect for the man who has been a prominent representative of the school since he first came to Notre Dame in 19... With the exception of a broken [...] suffered at Morningside, [...] the star has been remarkably free [...] and his exhibition [...] this year was one of the [...] performances in [...]

Was 25 Years Old.

GEORGE GIPP, NOTRE DAME GRID STAR, IS DEAD

Mother, Brother and Sister at Bedside When End Comes in South Bend Hospital.

Special Dispatch to The Chicago Evening American.

SOUTH BEND, Ind., Dec. 14.—George Gipp, star halfback of the undefeated Notre Dame football team, died here early today following a three weeks' illness of streptococcic throat trouble. Gipp's mother, brother and sister were at his bedside when death occurred.

Gipp was 24 years old. Three weeks ago he became ill of tonsilitis, which developed into pneumonia. Many of his teammates and fellow students offered their blood for transfusion, but Gipp was too weak to undergo the operation.

PICKED FOR ALL-AMERICAN.

At the end of the present football season Gipp was picked by all experts for halfback on the All-American team.

BATTLES DEATH TO LAST.

Just as he battled on the gridiron, Gipp fought with iron determination against death to the last. Physicians worked over him for hours in a desperate effort to prolong the life of the dying athlete. Gipp was rational throughout his last hours and with gritted teeth and clenched fists he struggled with his foe.

Mrs. Matthew Gipp, his mother, swooned when she learned last night [...] was dying. Revived [...]

REQUISCAT
By R. S.

Ah, lad, 'tis over now, and now you see
The road that takes you home when work's well done;
Methinks it meet to believe that you have won
The final and the greatest victory;
The universe's rhythm and the din
Of trumpets greet you as you near the goal.
Sorb and Dinmick stand to meet your soul.
While here below, beneath a clouded sun,
Wide-eyed and silent fellows move about,
Scourged to the soul by icy Death's stern knout,
Partaking in the death that claimed their One.
Lo! how the tear-drops gleam as Notre Dame
Opens her heart and writes therein your name!

George Gipp's death sent the Notre Dame campus and fans all across the country into mourning on the very day he was named a Walter Camp All-American.

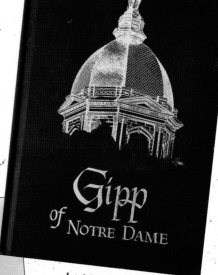

Gipp of Notre Dame

In 1954, James Peterson wrote *Gipp of Notre Dame*, a book documenting the life of George Gipp.

Because of his all-around talent, his popularity, and his death at a young age, George Gipp stands alone as the most legendary player in the history of Notre Dame football.

KNUTE ROCKNE
ALL AMERICAN
NOTRE DAME CLUB
DINNER
OCT. 24, 1940

RONALD

PAT O'BRIEN

Ronald Reagan (as George Gipp) and Pat O'Brien (as Knute Rockne) were honored with patches for their roles in *Knute Rockne All American*.

The Four Horsemen

"Outlined against a blue-gray October sky, the Four Horsemen rode again. In dramatic lore they are known as famine, pestilence, destruction, and death. These are only aliases. Their real names are: Stuhldreher, Miller, Crowley, and Layden."

With that famous prose, Grantland Rice opened his *New York Herald–Tribune* article documenting Notre Dame's 13–7 win over Army at the Polo Grounds on October 18, 1924. The legendary sportswriter had no idea of the lasting impact his words would have on generations of football fans.

More than 80 years later, American sports fans are able to conjure the names of the Four Horsemen of Notre Dame more easily than those of the biblical Four Horsemen of the Apocalypse. Certainly, that is a testament to Rice's immortal words. It also speaks to the salesmanship of Notre Dame coach Knute Rockne, who used the moniker to tout his backfield as the best in the land, and to the creativity of George Strickler, the student publicist who answered a newspaper request for a photo of the players by posing them on horses, creating one of the most effective publicity shots in sports history. Wire services distributed the photo nationwide, ensuring a lasting legacy for the Four Horsemen and their school.

Those who watched them play will insist that the Four Horsemen were not the product of brilliant writing or a catchy marketing campaign. It was their dominance on the field—the wide range of skills that prompted Rice to describe that game against Army in the manner he did—that allowed Harry Stuhldreher, Don Miller, Jim Crowley, and Elmer Layden to leave opposing players trying to corral the wind in ways that defied the traditional power-running style favored by teams of their era.

None of the Horsemen weighed more than 165 pounds or stood taller than six feet, but each stood out. All four

Perhaps the most famous publicity photo in the history of college sports introduced America to the faces of the Four Horsemen—(from left) Don Miller, Elmer Layden, Jim Crowley, and Harry Stuhldreher.

earned All-American honors. All four became coaches and were enshrined in the College Football Hall of Fame, located in South Bend.

Stuhldreher, the quarterback, was a born leader, an accurate passer, and an effective blocker despite his 5'7", 151-pound frame. He hailed from Massillon, Ohio, and won the starting job as a sophomore.

> "Our record helped, too. If we'd lost a couple, I don't think we would have been remembered."
>
> —Jim Crowley

Miller also hailed from Ohio, having followed three older brothers to South Bend. Harry "Red" Miller was one of Notre Dame's first stars, but Don was an even better breakaway threat. Rockne called him the best open-field runner he ever coached.

Crowley was directed to South Bend from Green Bay, Wisconsin, by Packers founder Curly Lambeau, his high school coach and a Notre Dame alum. "Sleepy Jim" was a shifty runner with supreme confidence. Facing a critical third-and-ten in the 1924 win over Army, Crowley called timeout, stepped off the yardage needed, and exclaimed to his teammates, "It's only ten yards. A truck horse could run that far."

The Iowa-born Layden, who went on to coach the Fighting Irish from 1934 to 1940, was the fastest of the Horsemen, able to cover 100 yards in less than 10 seconds.

Other All-Americans of the Era

The era from 1918 to 1940 was packed with as many big names as any other time in Notre Dame football history. First names were not even necessary in many cases. Everyone knew Rockne, Gipp, and those famous Four Horsemen: Stuhldreher, Miller, Crowley, and Layden.

In 1929 and 1930, quarterback Frank Carideo (pictured) became Notre Dame's first two-time consensus All-American when he was named as a first-team choice on every ballot in the land. "He could run, pass, and kick," noted Rockne, and he led the 1929 team to an undefeated record despite playing all nine games on the road while a new stadium was being built.

Halfback Marchy Schwartz was one of three All-Americans nominated from the 1930 squad. He became a consensus pick again in 1931, as did tackles Joe Kurth in 1932 and Ed Beinor in 1938.

He told Rockne he was too light to play fullback when asked to do so in 1922 but gave it a try and, ultimately, brought a new dimension to the position. His timely interceptions helped the Notre Dame defense become a force in its own right. He also handled the punting chores.

Together, the quartet gave foes nightmares. They would start in a conventional formation, race into position via the "Rockne shift," and then it was anyone's guess which one would end up with the ball. Their speed and finesse, behind the blocking of a relatively light but fierce supporting cast known as the "Seven Mules," led the 1924 team to a 10–0 record and Notre Dame's first national championship.

Left: As successful as the Four Horsemen were, it was the up-front blocking of the "Seven Mules"—(left to right) Ed Hunsinger, Edgar "Rip" Miller, Noble Kizer, Adam Walsh, Johnny Weibel, Joe Bach, and Chuck Collins—that opened gaping holes in opposing defenses.

1924: A National Title

In November 1962, nearly 38 years after the Four Horsemen made their final ride for the Fighting Irish, columnist Bob Curran wrote, "The 1924 Notre Dame team was the most colorful football team ever assembled. It contributed more to football than any other team."

His contention (one that has numerous supporters) was that Notre Dame's fast-paced attack, backfield motion, and liberal use of the forward pass during a 10–0 season changed the way the game was played. It was the year of the Four Horsemen and the Seven Mules. Knute Rockne called it his favorite team.

En route to the first bowl game in Notre Dame history—a Rose Bowl date with Stanford—the Fighting Irish players were a well-dressed and talented bunch.

NOTRE DAME UNIVERSITY'S UNBEATEN FOOTBALL TEAM AT ILLINOIS CENTRAL STATION CHICAGO EN ROUTE TO CALIFORNIA VIA NEW ORLEANS DECEMBER 20TH 1924

The Veteran Athletes' Association of Philadelphia awarded Notre Dame the Eugene C. Bonniwell Trophy for its 1924 national championship.

Knute Rockne knew he was coaching a powerhouse. Notre Dame's only loss the previous season came at the hands of a talented Nebraska squad, and the Four Horsemen were now seniors.

The schedule opened with back-to-back shutouts of overmatched Lombard and Wabash before the Irish headed to New York's Polo Grounds to face an Army team loaded with All-Americans. As well known as Grantland Rice's "Four Horsemen" quote would become, it was the next paragraph in his report on that 13–7 game that truly captured the might of the Irish:

"When the cyclone starts from South Bend, where the candle lights still gleam through the Indiana sycamores," the famous sportswriter warned, "those in the way must take to the storm cellars at top speed."

A second trip out east produced a 12–0 blanking of Princeton, and Notre Dame then rattled off consecutive routs of Georgia Tech, Wisconsin, and Nebraska. The Cartier Field crowd that watched the Irish avenge their 1923 loss to Nebraska was said to have exceeded stadium capacity by several thousand.

A 13–6 win over Northwestern before 45,000 fans at Chicago's Soldier Field and a 40–19 romp of Carnegie Tech completed a 9–0 regular season, earning the Irish a Rose Bowl invitation. In Pasadena, Stanford was no match, and Notre Dame's 27–10 victory left no doubt. Those colorful Irish were 1924 national champions.

Notre Dame's First Rose Bowl: January 1, 1925

Getting to a bowl game was no small feat for the 1924 Fighting Irish. Sure, their perfect record, star power, and popular coach made them an attractive opponent. But the Rose Bowl was the only bowl game in existence at the time, and travel to Pasadena, California, was no routine matter. Still, Knute Rockne helped Notre Dame sort out the details, and the school accepted an invitation to take on Stanford, coached by Pop Warner and led by fullback Ernie Nevers.

It was a battle of the unbeatens for the national title. The "Rockne shift" went head-to-head against Warner's double wingbacks and unbalanced line. The speed and finesse of the Four Horsemen squared off against the power-running of Nevers, a bruising, 205-pound locomotive.

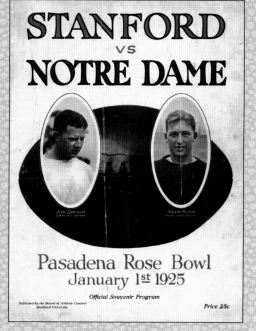

But it was Elmer Layden who stole the show. The speedster scored three touchdowns—two covering at least 70 yards—and the Irish made a mighty goal-line stand in the second half, stopping Nevers on a fourth-down plunge from eight inches short of the goal line. The final score: Notre Dame 27, Stanford 10.

Captains Jim Lawson of Stanford (left) and Adam Walsh of Notre Dame were the cover boys on the 1925 Rose Bowl program.

Although a handful of bowl games sprang up in the 1930s—including the Orange Bowl, the Sugar Bowl, and the Cotton Bowl—it would be 45 years before Notre Dame, wanting its players to focus on their late-semester studies, would accept another bid.

Notre Dame Stadium

Sadly, the "House that Rockne Built" served as the workplace for the man most responsible for its existence for only one season. It was the success of Knute Rockne's 1920s Notre Dame teams that begged for the building of a more spacious home than the less-than-30,000-capacity Cartier Field. As fate would have it, Notre Dame Stadium's 1930 debut season was Rockne's last before the plane crash that ended his life.

Rockne's hand, however, can still be seen in its confines today. He supervised the design of the parking system that remains largely intact. So if you find yourself stuck in the back of a slow-moving parade while driving to a Notre Dame home game, you know whom to curse. But before you do so, consider that it was also Rock who lobbied against having a track circle the field because he wanted the stands close to the sidelines for better views of the action and a more intimate feel—traits that still contribute to one of the most electric atmospheres in all of college football.

Bids arrived from prominent contractors across the country in 1929. The Osborn Engineering Company, which counted Chicago's Comiskey Park and New York's Polo Grounds and Yankee Stadium among its masterpieces, won the job.

The mammoth Michigan Stadium in Ann Arbor served as a blueprint, though Notre Dame's was built smaller and with an end zone tunnel, rather than one at midfield. More than two million bricks, 400 tons of steel, and 15,000 cubic yards of concrete contributed to the final

cost of more than $750,000. Capacity was initially 54,000, though more than 59,000 fans soon started packing Notre Dame Stadium's wooden bleachers.

Excavation of the site took place in the summer of 1929, and construction began the following April. On October 4, 1930, Notre Dame squared off against Southern Methodist for the first game on the Kentucky bluegrass that had been transplanted from Cartier Field—another Rockne touch. The official dedication had been set for the following week's matchup against Navy, perhaps explaining why fewer than 15,000 fans watched the Fighting Irish's 20–14 opening win.

One week later, South Bend celebrated. Rockne spoke eloquently. A eulogy for late Fighting Irish All-American George Gipp was given by Notre Dame's president, Father Charles L. O'Donnell. And administrators and benefactors were thanked as more than 40,000 turned out to watch the Fighting Irish dominate the Midshipmen 26–2, at a venue that would become one of the most storied in American sports.

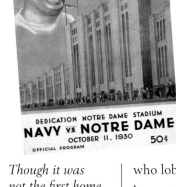

Though it was not the first home game at Notre Dame Stadium, the 1930 contest with rival Navy was designated as the "dedication game."

Right: *The bulk of the work required to construct Notre Dame Stadium took place in a four-month span beginning in April 1930.*

Knute Rockne coached only one season at Notre Dame Stadium— the "House that Rockne Built." Here he kicks things off with a speech to the crowd during that 1930 campaign.

The Fighting Irish

Long before the leprechaun mascot appeared in South Bend, a series of Irish terriers served in that role.

In the 1800s, they were called Catholics, for obvious reasons. Also in the early era, some took to calling Notre Dame's football players "Ramblers" or "Rovers" for their willingness to travel the country to take on willing opponents. How they came to be known as the Fighting Irish is a matter of some debate, though Notre Dame president Reverend Matthew Walsh formally adopted the nickname in 1927.

During an 1899 game at Northwestern, fans of the Evanston, Illinois, school were said to have chanted "Kill the Fighting Irish! Kill the Fighting Irish!" as their Wildcats were down 5–0 against Notre Dame at halftime. Another account of the nickname's origin had a Notre Dame player yelling at his teammates at halftime of a 1909 game against Michigan, "What's the matter with you guys? You're all Irish, and you're not fighting worth a lick." After Notre Dame rallied for its first triumph over the Wolverines, the press declared it "a victory for the Fighting Irish."

Whomever you believe initiated it, there is little doubt that newspapers led to the school's decision to adopt the name officially. Francis Wallace, a Notre Dame graduate, used the moniker liberally in the *New York Daily News* in the 1920s. If opposing fans sometimes shouted the nickname in a derogatory manner, those in blue and gold took it squarely as a nod to their tenacity.

So with "Fighting Irish" as a nickname, where does a school turn for its mascot? For more than 40 years, the answer was a four-legged one. Several sources cite an Irish terrier named Tipperary Terrence (and later Tipperary Terrence II) serving as the first team mascot starting in 1924. Brick Top Shuan-Rhu took the reins in 1930, and a series of Irish terriers named Clashmore Mike held the honor from 1933 until the mid-1960s. A photo of the 1924 national championship squad shows Elmer Layden in the front row holding not a Rose Bowl trophy but team mascot Tipperary Terrence II.

The leprechaun did not become the official mascot until 1965, but the spirit of his raised fists had clearly been manifested in the "Fighting Irish" nickname decades earlier. From Norwegian coach Knute Rockne to his players of German, Italian, Irish, or other descent, Notre Dame turned what was intended as an insult into a legacy.

"While given in irony," reported school publication *Scholastic* in a 1929 edition, "[the Fighting Irish nickname] has become our heritage."

Below left: *Notre Dame's four-legged mascots in the mid-1900s were so popular, some even warranted official school news releases.*

Prefatory Note

NOTRE DAME, Indiana (News Release)—The fortunes of the Notre Dame football team during the football season will be aided and abetted by the presence of a new mascot, Shannon View Mike I, an Irish terrier. He was presented to the team by James McGarraghy, Chicago business man and long time follower of the Irish, and was received in behalf of the team by Co-Captain Jim Martin.

Shannon View Mike I is the third mascot for the Fighting Irish in modern times. His two predecessors were also Irish terriers. Clashmore Mike I was given to the team by a Chicago kennel owner in 1935. He died in 1945 with 10 years of varsity football experience. He was buried in the Notre Dame stadium. Clashmore Mike II, who was also presented by Mr. McGarraghy, joined the team in 1945. He disappeared from his home in the stadium on the eve of the 1948 Notre Dame-Navy game and has not been seen since.

The first two names of the new mascot are derived from the fact that he comes from the Shannon View Kennel in Chicago.

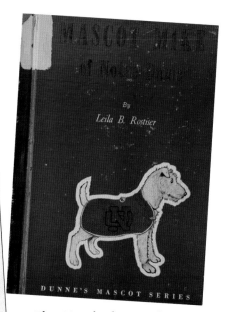

This 1949 book, part of a series on mascots, was a 64-page celebration of Notre Dame's Irish terrier.

National Titles in 1929 and 1930

Right: *An artist portrayed this USC player winning the attention of the ladies before Notre Dame's game against the Trojans in 1929, but it was the Fighting Irish who prevailed in a 13–12 battle before 112,000-plus fans at Soldier Field.*

Knute Rockne called 1928 "the worst season Notre Dame has ever seen." Though the Fighting Irish "won one for The Gipper," they lost four games for the first time since 1905. The coach vowed to show the college football world that he and Notre Dame were far from through.

The year 1929 was memorable on several fronts. After the stock market crashed on October 29, many Americans turned to sports as a welcome relief from their daily misery. The Irish were facing a schedule without a home game, as Cartier Field had been excavated and the new stadium was under construction. And they were tackling that schedule with an ill coach. Before the opener at Indiana University, Rockne had contracted phlebitis, an inflammation of a vein in the leg that can be associated with life-threatening blood clots. Doctors advised him to give up coaching. Rockne, of course, would follow no such advice.

Instructing the team from a hospital bed, reclining wheelchair, and even via telephone at times, Rockne steered a team with a dominant line, the speedy running of Jack Elder, the punishing blocking of fullback Marty Brill, and All-American quarterback Frank Carideo to a 9–0 record. The closest call was a 13–12 win against Southern Cal before more than 112,000 fans at Soldier Field, as the Trojans missed an extra point. A 7–0 blanking of Army on a bitter November afternoon at Yankee Stadium secured a national championship. The Fighting Irish had overcome all odds.

Rockne was back on his feet in 1930, barking from the sideline of a new stadium. His veteran team celebrated by conquering a ten-game schedule, outscoring foes 265–74 to repeat as national champions. For the second straight season, an extra point at Soldier Field loomed large. The Irish blocked one late to pull out a 7–6 victory over Army in front of 110,000-plus patrons. Seven players from that team—Rockne's last—were named All-Americans during their time at Notre Dame.

Knute Rockne frequently coached from a wheelchair during his last two seasons in 1929 and '30. His Fighting Irish won the final 19 games under their legendary coach's guidance.

What Makes a National Title?

Hot debate about the national championship of college football is not a new phenomenon. If the recently adopted and ever-changing Bowl Championship Series has not appeased fans who clamor for a playoff system, imagine how those same fans might have reacted in 1920, when the Park H. Davis ratings had 9–0 Notre Dame and 6–0–1 Princeton sharing the crown, with the First Interstate Bank Athletic Foundation recognizing 9–0 California as the champion. Confused? You're not alone.

Many publications, polls, and rating systems have chosen the NCAA Division I champion over the years. Since its inception in 1936, the Associated Press poll of sportswriters—the most universally recognized—has honored Notre Dame as national champion eight times. Oklahoma stands second with seven.

Other sources that have been factored into "consensus" national title designations include the coaches' poll, the Football Writers Association of America, and the National Football Foundation and Hall of Fame. Notre Dame is generally considered to have won 11 consensus national titles, more than any other school.

Post-Rockne: Following a Giant

Less than a week after Knute Rockne's April 4, 1931, funeral, and with spring practice looming, hearts were heavy in South Bend. Notre Dame felt it was important to get on with the business of preparing for the fall season, but under whose watch?

The job of replacing college football's ultimate coach was not going to be easy. It could have fallen to one of the many Rockne disciples who were leading other programs throughout the country. Largely in the interest of maintaining continuity, it was given to a man Rockne had called "the best line coach in America."

Heartley "Hunk" Anderson had played pro football and served as head coach at the University of St. Louis for two years. His best work, though, came in molding Notre Dame's lines into some of the finest in the country under Rockne. Anderson was promoted to "senior" coach, while Jack Chevigny, just two years removed from his days in the backfield, would serve in a "junior" capacity.

That settled, a record 320 students tried out for the team that year, certainly a tribute to the memory of Rockne. Anderson's debut was a 25–0 Irish romp at Indiana University, but a scoreless tie against Northwestern the following week ended Notre Dame's 20-game winning streak. In November, the Irish suffered their first loss since 1928 when Southern Cal rallied from a 14–0 deficit to prevail 16–14. It was one of the greatest comebacks in the early history of college football, and it took a lot out of the Fighting Irish, who were shut out by Army in the finale a week later.

Following a second straight two-loss season in 1932, Anderson's boys slipped to 3–5–1 in 1933. Both he and Athletic Director Jesse Harper, the former Irish coach who had left his Kansas ranch to guide the department after Rockne's death, stepped down. Elmer Layden of Four Horsemen fame was hired to handle both positions, and he oversaw a rebirth of the school's winning tradition.

Layden was a popular choice, having compiled a 48–16–6 record in seven seasons at Duquesne in Pittsburgh. After a 7–6 loss to Texas in 1934, in Layden's first game as coach of his alma mater, Notre Dame won six of its final eight. And though his Irish never claimed a national title, none of Layden's next six teams lost more than twice. He resigned after the 1940 campaign, later taking over as commissioner of the National Football League.

Before opening the 1931 regular season, Notre Dame scrimmaged in the "Rockne Memorial Game" as a tribute to their late head coach.

Elmer Layden coached the Fighting Irish to a 47–13–3 record over seven seasons from 1934 to 1940.

Jesse Harper (left) returned to Notre Dame from his Kansas farm following Knute Rockne's death and oversaw a football program coached by Heartley "Hunk" Anderson (right).

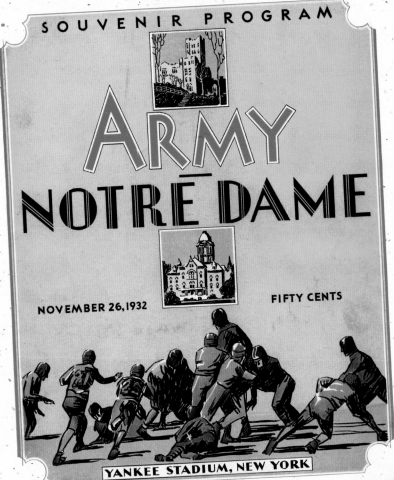

SOUVENIR PROGRAM

ARMY
NOTRE DAME

NOVEMBER 26, 1932   FIFTY CENTS

YANKEE STADIUM, NEW YORK

FOOTBALL
1938

UNIVERSITY OF
NOTRE DAME
1938 Football Schedule

OCT. 1 — KANSAS AT NOTRE DAME
OCT. 8 — GEORGIA TECH AT ATLANTA
OCT. 15 — ILLINOIS AT NOTRE DAME
OCT. 22 — CARNEGIE TECH AT NOTRE DAME
OCT. 29 — ARMY AT NEW YORK
NOV. 5 — NAVY AT BALTIMORE
NOV. 12 — MINNESOTA AT NOTRE DAME
NOV. 19 — NORTHWESTERN AT EVANSTON
DEC. 3 — SOUTHERN CAL. AT LOS ANGELES

Ticket sale to individual games will open August 1st. ● Season ticket sale for home games will open June 20th.

As this pocket schedule shows, the 1938 Fighting Irish outscored their opponents by a cumulative score of 149–39.

The Fighting Irish avenged a last-minute 1931 loss to Army during their return trip to Yankee Stadium one year later. Notre Dame shut out the Cadets by a 21–0 score.

This leather helmet was signed by members of the 1934 Fighting Irish, who posted a 6–3 record in Elmer Layden's debut as Notre Dame head coach.

The Fighting Irish and Joe Savoldi, Notre Dame's leading rusher in 1929, made Carnegie Tech one of ten victims in 1930.

NOTRE DAME STADIUM, Oct. 18, 1930

"JUMPING JOE" SAVOLDI — FULL BACK

| Notre Dame | 21 |
| Carnegie Tech. | 6 |

1933
NOTRE DAME FOOTBALL SCHEDULE

Oct. 7 — Kansas at Notre Dame
Oct. 14 — Indiana at Bloomington
Oct. 21 — Carnegie Tech at Pittsburgh
Oct. 28 — Pittsburgh at Notre Dame
Nov. 4 — Navy at Baltimore
Nov. 11 — Purdue at Notre Dame
Nov. 18 — Northwestern at Evanston
Nov. 25 — Southern California at Notre Dame
Dec. 2 — Army at New York

Early Orders Get Better Seats

RITE TODAY FOR TICKET PLICATION BLANKS

The 1933 season was an unusual one indeed in South Bend. In going 3–5–1, the Fighting Irish did not win a single game on their home field.

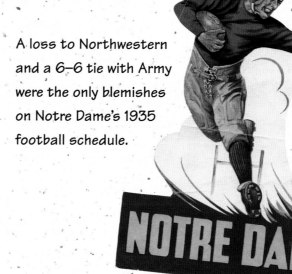

A loss to Northwestern and a 6–6 tie with Army were the only blemishes on Notre Dame's 1935 football schedule.

1935
NOTRE DAME FOOTBALL SCHEDULE

SEPT. 28
Kansas at Notre Dame
OCT. 5
Carnegie Tech at Pittsburgh
OCT. 12
Wisconsin at Madison
OCT. 19
Pittsburgh at Notre Dame
OCT. 26
Navy at Baltimore
NOV. 2
Ohio State at Columbus
NOV. 9
Northwestern at Notre Dame
NOV. 16
Army at New York
NOV. 23 — Southern California at Notre Dame

Early Orders Get Better Seats

WRITE TODAY FOR TICKET APPLICATION BLANKS

SOUTHERN METHODIST
VS
NOTRE DAME

NOTRE DAME STADIUM   OCTOBER 4 1930

GATE 4
SECTION 8
ROW 28
SEAT

NAVY
VS
NOTRE DAME

DEDICATION
NOTRE DAME STADIUM   OCTOBER 11 1930

2 P.M.   ADMIT ONE   PRICE $5.00

GATE 4
SECTION 8
ROW 19
SEAT

The interlocking N and D were a staple of 1920s Notre Dame apparel, just as they are today.

Though Southern Methodist was the first opponent to play at the newly opened Notre Dame Stadium, the following week's date with rival Navy was deemed the dedication game.

Honoring the
NOTRE DAME
1920
Foot Ball Team

OLIVER HOTEL
November 23 1920

A banquet for the 1920 Notre Dame football team was held two days before the Fighting Irish capped a perfect 9–0 season with a 25–0 shutout of Michigan State.

The Game of the Century

Play-by-play charts were a bit more primitive and artistic in 1935 than they are today, but fans could relive Notre Dame's 18–13 victory over Ohio State with the one below.

The most anticipated game of the 1935 season was not living up to the hype. Notre Dame did not belong on the same field as Ohio State through the first three quarters in Columbus. More than 81,000 fans, some of whom had paid $50 or more for tickets, were witnessing a thrashing on November 2. It appeared that those who chanted "Catholics, go home!" upon Notre Dame's arrival had gotten their wish, as the visitors were virtual no-shows after falling behind 13–0 entering the final 15 minutes in the battle of unbeatens.

Then, lightning struck. Not literally, but in the form of a Fighting Irish comeback that produced an 18–13 win and set this game apart in the annals of college football.

According to the *Chicago Tribune*, "No Notre Dame team has written a more brilliant page in football history than these boys today. Beaten 13–0 in three periods of play, Notre Dame, almost without warning, rose with tornadic fury."

Recounted *The New York Times*, "The incredible happened . . . so fast and furiously as the lion-hearted blue-shirted players from South Bend became so many swirling, insensate fire-eaters as to leave the vast assemblage stunned."

But it was an unlikely hero who emerged to turn this rout into a classic. Coach Elmer Layden gave an inspired halftime talk about Joe Sullivan, the team captain who had died earlier that year from pneumonia. Then he turned to a second-string group that included Andy Pilney, who replaced All-American halfback Bill Shakespeare, and roused Notre Dame from its slumber.

Pilney made a 28-yard punt return on the last play of the third quarter to spark a rally, then completed a pass to Frank Gaul to the one-yard line to set up Notre Dame's first touchdown. Pilney then connected with Mike Layden, the coach's younger brother, on a 15-yard touchdown toss. Failed conversions after those scores, though, left Notre Dame trailing 13–12 with less than two minutes remaining.

However, Ohio State did not have a chance to run out the clock. On the Buckeyes' next play from scrimmage, Dick Beltz fumbled and the Irish fell on the ball near midfield. Fans held their breath as Pilney, receivers covered, improvised with his feet and ran 32 yards. He was knocked out of bounds so hard that a stretcher was needed to get him to the locker room. Shakespeare trotted in and lobbed a pass into the end zone, where Wayne Millner made the catch for the winning score.

Fifteen years later, sportswriters voted it "the Game of the Century."

This 1935 program commemorated Notre Dame's first-ever game against Ohio State with a clever blending of scarlet and green.

Chart Shows Ohio–N. D. Play-by-Play

OHIO STATE vs. NOTRE DAME

Chart by Noel Holmes.

Game Day

On November 26, 1927, Notre Dame and Southern Cal set a college football attendance record that still stands, as more than 120,000 raucous fans packed the seats of Soldier Field to watch the Fighting Irish pull out a 7–6 victory.

The years between World Wars I and II saw explosive growth in Notre Dame's football fan base, largely due to Knute Rockne and the national championship success that the colorful coach brought to South Bend. Increased ticket demand led to the building of Notre Dame Stadium in 1930, which nearly doubled capacity at home games to more than 50,000. But nowhere was the growing popularity of the Fighting Irish more evident than in nearby Chicago.

The South Shore Line between South Bend and Chicago was a godsend in 1929, when the Irish played three games at Soldier Field and one at Northwestern while Notre Dame Stadium was being built.

More than 120,000 spectators took in a 1928 game against Navy at Soldier Field. The following year, Soldier Field crowds of 90,000 (Wisconsin) and 112,912 (USC) watched the Irish. And in 1930, while the first game ever played at Notre Dame Stadium drew just 14,751 fans, a 7–6 win against Army on November 29 attracted 110,000 to Soldier Field. Folks in the Windy City were going crazy about the football program 90 miles to the east.

Not coincidentally, the concept of "subway alumni"—faithful followers of Notre Dame

Crowds in excess of 100,000 fans were not unusual when Notre Dame suited up at Chicago's Soldier Field in the 1920s and '30s.

who did not attend the school—emerged in this same era. But these fans were not limited to Chicago or the Midwest. *New York Daily News* columnist Paul Gallico wrote of the Irish's popularity among thousands in New York City in the 1930s:

"The annual visit of the football team of the University of Notre Dame to New York for the football game with West Point brings about the... gathering of that amazing clan of self-appointed Notre Dame alumni which will whoop and rage and rant and roar through our town from sunup until long after sundown... in honor of a school to which they never went.... And this business is a phenomenon purely for this one game. There are no self-appointed Colgate... or Tulane or Purdue alumni when those teams come to visit our town."

More than 112,000 fans packed into Soldier Field to watch the Fighting Irish beat Southern Cal 13–12 in 1929.

Knute Rockne All American

The spirit of Notre Dame's greatest coach lives on with every airing of *Knute Rockne All American*, the 1940 film starring Pat O'Brien as Rockne and a young Ronald Reagan as George Gipp. Even nonfans are likely to have caught scenes from the motion picture that some consider a classic. Norman Chad, who explained in a 2005 *Washington Post* column that he grew up hating the Fighting Irish, went on to say that watching *Knute Rockne All American* changed his outlook.

"You hear Knute's father, Lars, tell Knute about America: 'It's big enough for anything, son, or for anybody,'" Chad wrote. "'That's why we're going there.' He made me want to immigrate here all over again."

The great things Rockne did after deciding to attend Notre Dame, and later coach football there, are the focus of the movie, which was shot just a few years after Rockne died in a 1931 plane crash.

Bonnie Rockne—Knute's widow—and Notre Dame administrators were thrilled with the screenplay written by Robert Buckner. The casting turned out to be a bit trickier. At first, they were not enamored with O'Brien, the handsome James Cagney sidekick who was of Irish descent. How would he capture the magic of Rockne, a fiery Norwegian who favored desire and hard work over charm? Nevertheless, O'Brien won them over. He nailed

Pat O'Brien, playing the lead role in 1940's Knute Rockne All American, *introduced a generation of Notre Dame fans to Rockne's "Win One for The Gipper" speech.*

Pat O'Brien, as Knute Rockne, coaches Ronald Reagan, as George Gipp, in the 1940 film Knute Rockne All American.

South Bend was the place to be for the 1940 premiere of Knute Rockne All American. *Stars Ronald Reagan and Pat O'Brien were among several luminaries at the initial screening.*

Rockne's voice and later called the role his favorite in an acting career that spanned six decades.

The film's "Win One for The Gipper" speech is its defining moment, but viewers also meet Rockne the aspiring chemist, the famed Four Horsemen, and witness—with the aid of newsreel footage—the early success of Notre Dame football.

The first movie ever filmed on the Notre Dame campus, *Knute Rockne All American* is preserved in the Library of Congress's National Film Registry as "culturally significant." Of course, Notre Dame fans don't have to be convinced of that.

This program for the world premiere of Knute Rockne All American *is autographed by Ronald Reagan, who portrayed George Gipp and 40 years later became President of the United States.*

President Gipp

Now starting at halfback... the President of the United States. Two-term president Ronald Reagan's portrayal of "The Gipper" in the 1940 film *Knute Rockne All American* only served to further the mystique of Notre Dame football.

Reagan, a former radio sportscaster, starred in more than 50 films, the first in 1937. And although the Rockne film didn't earn any Oscar nominations, no role stuck with Reagan quite like the fun-loving and talented George Gipp, whom he brought to life on the silver screen almost 20 years after Notre Dame lost the All-American at age 25.

Through his successful run as California governor and his two presidential terms in the 1980s, it was not unusual for Reagan to be referred to as "The Gipper." He returned to South Bend in 1988 to introduce a Knute Rockne stamp being issued by the U.S. Postal Service. And he once urged Vice President George H. W. Bush to "Go out there and win one for The Gipper."

Ronald Reagan, a fine athlete himself as a youth, did not need a stunt double to execute a kicking scene as Notre Dame's George Gipp in Knute Rockne All American.

This original script for Knute Rockne All American *shows that the working title was somewhat less memorable than the one chosen for the 1940 classic.*

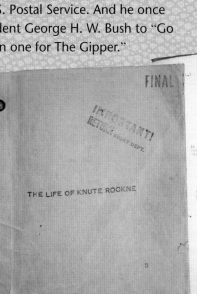

STANFORD
vs.
NOTRE-DAME

FOOTBALL GAME
PASADENA ROSE BOWL
JANUARY 1, 1925
Price 25¢

The cover of this 1925 Rose Bowl program seemed to favor Stanford, given the shades of black and red. But the Irish prevailed 27–10 to claim the national championship.

The Los Angeles Times

Weather: Warm.

LOS ANGELES, CAL., JAN. 1, 1925

Extra Edition

NOTRE DAME OVERLAYDENS STANFORD

CALIFORNIA IS SCENE OF HARDEST CONTEST

Notre Dame's Conquest of the West Gives Undisputed Claim to National Honors.

PASADENA, Calif., Jan. 1.— Like two struggling giants these champions of football, Notre Dame and Stanford, fought beneath the warm California sun.

It was not an easy victory for the giant from Notre Dame. Stanford fought, and fought hard. Never, until the last few minutes of play was the conquest of the West assured to these plucky,— and smart, warriors of the East. Never, and the reason was Nevers. He was in himself almost the whole offense of the western team and, against a less worthy opponent, he must have prevailed. But there were times when Stanford left the ground and took the air. Then they learned that Notre Dame too had a great fullback, one Elmer Layden.

The day was one of glory for Elmer. Twice, when the Stanford offensive was in full swing, he leaped into the air, firmly grasped the ball that was speeding to a Stanford man doomed to disappointment, and raced away on wings of the wind for a touchdown. And it was a glorious day for Huntsinger. The alert end gave Layden flawless interference, and himself added to the score by recovering a Stanford fumble and galloping off across the goal line. Glory came too to Crowley, who scored the first touchdown of the game, and to Stuhldreher, who fought gamely until an injury forced him to retire, and to Don Miller. But the greatest glory was that of the line, from end to end. When Nevers had carried the ball to the one yard seemed...

Top, Elmer Layden, the Horseman who took the bit in his mouth at Stanford. Lower left, John McMullen, left tackle. Lower right, Ed Huntsinger, who recovered a Stanford fumble for a touchdown. Action picture shows "em pilin' up" at Stanford.

The Los Angeles Times described the 1925 Rose Bowl as a hard-fought "conquest of the West" by Notre Dame.

The 1924 Notre Dame squad won all nine games in the regular season and added a tenth victory against Stanford in the Rose Bowl—the first bowl game in Fighting Irish history.

FOOTBALL
Notre Dame vs Stanford

January 1st, 1925, 2:15 p. m.

ROSE BOWL Price $5.00 Tax Exempt

SEC. C
ENTER TUNNEL
ROW 16
SEAT 17
2
Notre Dame vs. Stanford
January 1, 1925, at 2:15 p. m.
ROSE BOWL, PASADENA
RETAIN THIS CHECK

A mere $5 was enough to snag a good seat to Notre Dame's first-ever bowl game on New Year's Day 1925. Some 53,000 fans bought tickets.

Georgia Tech was no match for Notre Dame on homecoming weekend in 1924. That year, few opponents were.

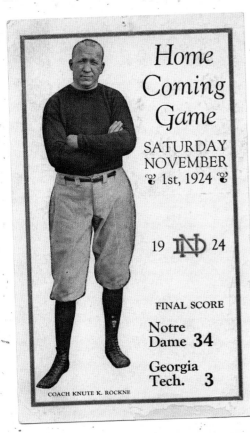

COACH KNUTE K. ROCKNE

Home Coming Game

SATURDAY NOVEMBER 1st, 1924

1924

FINAL SCORE

Notre Dame 34

Georgia Tech. 3

The 1924 Fighting Irish schedule might have looked like a gravestone to Notre Dame opponents. The Irish padded their overall victory margin with a 27–10 Rose Bowl win against Stanford.

19		24	
NOTRE DAME	40	LOMBARD	0
NOTRE DAME	34	WABASH	0
NOTRE DAME	13	ARMY	7
NOTRE DAME	12	PRINCETON	0
NOTRE DAME	34	GEORGIA T.	3
NOTRE DAME	38	WISCONSIN	3
NOTRE DAME	34	NEBRASKA	6
NOTRE DAME	13	N.WESTERN	6
NOTRE DAME	40	CARNEGIE T.	19
TOTAL	258	TOTAL	44

NOTRE DAME vs SOUTHERN CALIFORNIA

NOTRE DAME vs SOUTHERN CALIFORNIA

SOLDIER FIELD, CHICAGO
SATURDAY, NOVEMBER 26, 1927
PRICE 25 CENTS

Big crowds were the norm when Notre Dame played at Soldier Field. An estimated 120,000 were in attendance when the Fighting Irish edged Southern Cal 7–6 in the 1927 season finale.

This decal from the 1930s represents the end of the glory days of Knute Rockne.

NOTRE DAME

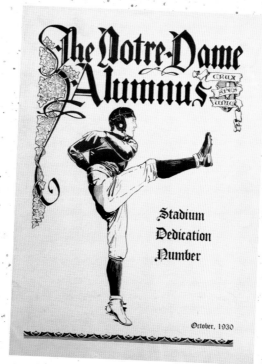

The Notre-Dame Alumnus

Stadium Dedication Number

October, 1930

This program marked the dedication of Notre Dame Stadium and kicked off Rockne's last season.

A prayer card from the funeral mass of Bonnie Rockne, who died June 2, 1956.

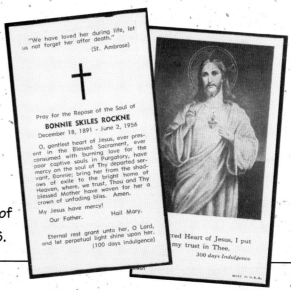

"We have loved her during life, let us not forget her after death."
(St. Ambrose)

Pray for the Repose of the Soul of
BONNIE SKILES ROCKNE
December 18, 1891 - June 2, 1956

O, gentlest heart of Jesus, ever present in the Blessed Sacrament, ever consumed with burning love for the poor captive souls in Purgatory, have mercy on the soul of Thy departed servant, Bonnie; bring her from the shadows of exile to the bright home of Heaven, where, we trust, Thou and Thy blessed Mother have woven for her a crown of unfading bliss. Amen.

My Jesus have mercy!
Our Father.   Hail Mary.

Eternal rest grant unto her, O Lord, and let perpetual light shine upon her.
(100 days indulgence)

...red Heart of Jesus, I put my trust in Thee.
300 days Indulgence

MADE IN U.S.A.

THE GOLDEN AGE
1941–1963

The 1940s were glorious years for Notre Dame, as the Irish produced four national championships, three Heisman Trophy winners, and the school's second coaching legend, Frank Leahy, before embarking on a 39-game unbeaten streak. Two more Heisman winners emerged in the 1950s from a campus that had become synonymous with college football excellence.

In one of the greatest games in college football history, Army All-American Hank Foldberg (left) prepares to take out Notre Dame's Bill Gompers on Army's four-yard line. This classic 1946 contest featured four Heisman Trophy winners and ended in a scoreless tie.

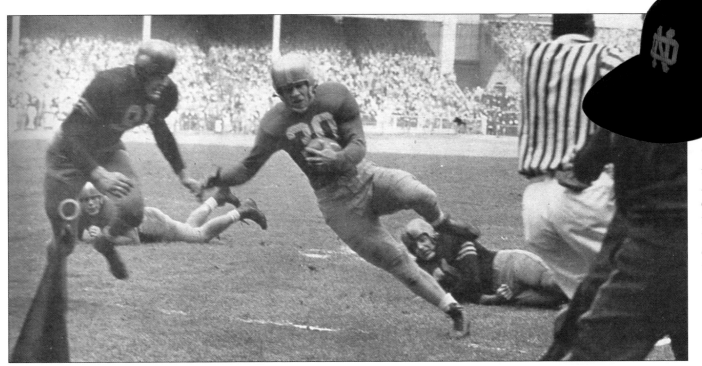

This cap was worn in the 1940s by Frank Leahy, who coached the Fighting Irish to six undefeated seasons and four consensus national titles.

Notre Dame's 41–7 rout of Navy in Baltimore in 1948 was part of a 39-game unbeaten string for the Irish.

Frank Leahy:
A New Coaching Legend Emerges

Frank Leahy grew up in a small South Dakota town called Winner. An apt name given the greatness Leahy would attain as Notre Dame's head football coach. His was a town, and a family, where hard work and steely resolve were the norm. His father was a farmer, freighter, and former pro wrestler who taught his four sons how to box. Frank also wrestled, learned the cowboy skills of riding and roping, and, by the time he reached his senior year at Winner High, was captain of the football, baseball, and basketball teams while serving as class president.

Frank Leahy signs his first contract as Notre Dame's head football coach in 1941, as Father Hugh O'Donnell, the university's president, looks on. Leahy was a 1931 graduate of the school and a tackle on Knute Rockne's last three Irish teams.

His football coach, Earl Walsh, had played on Knute Rockne's 1919 and 1920 Notre Dame teams and steered Leahy toward South Bend. Frank's older brother Gene had rewritten Creighton's football record books, but one look at Notre Dame's campus in the fall of 1927 told the younger Leahy he had made the right choice. He was small for a tackle, but his strong legs, hearty work habits, and quick thinking made him a Rockne favorite. Unfortunately, injuries limited Leahy's contributions. When a serious knee injury days before the 1930 opener devastated the senior, Rockne suggested that he serve as an assistant coach, setting a career course that would ultimately reward Leahy's alma mater.

Fast forward to January 1941. Since leaving South Bend, Leahy had assisted at Georgetown, worked as line coach under "Horseman" Jim Crowley at Michigan State and Fordham—where he tutored a guard named Vince Lombardi—and, in his head-coaching debut, led Boston College to a 20–2 two-year record and a 1941 Sugar Bowl victory (in only his second season at the helm). Now Notre Dame was beckoning him home. Leahy viewed it as the chance of a lifetime, and the Rockne protégé announced his arrival with as many syllables as he could muster: "The authorities at the University of Notre Dame saw fit to ask me to coach the football team at my alma mater," Leahy, the new head coach and athletic director, told his first group of Fighting Irish players. "My vocabulary lacks the words to describe fittingly the monumental feeling of joy which permeated my entire body and soul."

Leahy became something of a riddle to reporters. He was soft-spoken, tended to downplay the quality of his

> **"You know why Notre Dame is the best college team in the nation? It's because Frank Leahy is the greatest college coach who ever lived."**
>
> **—College and Pro Football Hall of Famer Harold "Red" Grange**

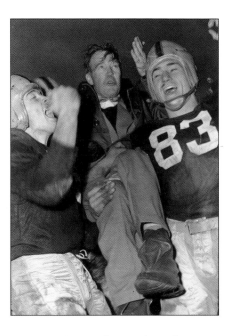

Frank Leahy is carried off the field by Don Penza in 1953, following the second-ranked Irish's 40–14 victory over SMU. It was the last game of Leahy's coaching career.

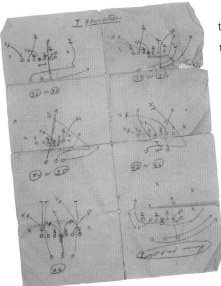

Leahy created an uproar when he scrapped Knute Rockne's box formation in favor of the T. Some of his plays involving the T-formation are shown here.

(Center): *Leahy temporarily left his coaching duties to enter the navy after the 1943 season.*

team, and frequently used larger words than necessary to get simple points across, a trait that may have dated back to his father's love for betting his friends that he could define any word in the dictionary. "I never saw him lose," Leahy noted.

With a background that taught him to work hard and demand perfection, a coaching foundation instilled by Rockne, and a position at Notre Dame that gave him access to the best players in the country, it's no wonder Leahy directed the Fighting Irish through one of the most dominant stretches in college football history.

Six of his teams went undefeated, including his first one in 1941 (8–0–1). Five claimed national championships, including four Associated Press titles in the 1940s. He took two years off to join the navy during World War II, but Leahy returned in 1946 and promptly led the Fighting Irish to a remarkable 39-game unbeaten string. Included was a run of 21 consecutive victories between 1946 and 1948. Four of his players won Heisman Trophies. Under Leahy, Notre Dame was strong, fast, and relentless.

Comparisons to Rockne were natural. That Leahy's record (87–11–9) did not pale in comparison to that of his mentor says volumes. The pupil may have lacked his teacher's charm, but his mind, his drive, and his compassion for his "lads" were familiar traits right up to the time Leahy stepped down in January 1954. He died of leukemia in 1973.

Changing Rockne's Offense

It was sacrilege. While the 1942 news headlines provided updates from World War II, the sports pages offered something nearly as eye-opening for Notre Dame fans. Frank Leahy was planning to abandon the time-tested "Rockne shift" in favor of the T-formation used by pro football's Chicago Bears and quarterback Sid Luckman.

Leahy wrote the book on the T-formation—literally.

Leahy's reasoning was sound, despite outcry from the Fighting Irish faithful. His best thrower, Angelo Bertelli, "couldn't run his way out of a paper bag," the coach would later say. Bertelli played halfback on the undefeated 1941 team, but Leahy moved him to quarterback to better showcase his strong and accurate arm.

Bertelli would take the ball directly from the center in the "T" and hand it to the faster backs behind him on running plays. When passing, Bertelli would drop back, allowing his linemen to form what Leahy called a protective "pocket," and aim for open receivers.

Bertelli won the 1943 Heisman Trophy from the T-formation, which helped Leahy's teams claim four consensus national titles and became college football's standard offensive set.

Leahy diagrams a play using the T-formation at a 1941 practice.

1943 National Title Season

During the 1943 season, several schools across the country suspended varsity play because of World War II. Those that continued would have players pressed into military duty before season's end. Quarterback Angelo Bertelli would begin the fall trying to help Notre Dame bounce back from a 7–2–2 record in 1942 and end it trying to help the Allies defeat Nazi Germany as a member of the Marine Corps.

Notre Dame set the tone for dominance early with a 41–0 drubbing of Pittsburgh, a 55–13 win over Georgia Tech, and a 35–12 victory at Michigan, in which Creighton Miller rushed for 159 yards and two scores on ten carries. Shutouts of Wisconsin (50–0) and Illinois (47–0) followed. No one, it seemed, could stop Leahy's lads.

The Fighting Irish faced adversity for the first time after a 33–6 rout of Navy on October 30. Two days later, with his marine training complete, Bertelli left for Parris Island. He had no way of knowing that his brilliant half-season of work would be enough to win him the Heisman Trophy,

The 9–1 Irish were unanimous national champions in 1943. The roster included Heisman Trophy winners Angelo Bertelli (48) and Johnny Lujack (32).

Creighton Miller

Creighton Miller lined up behind Heisman Trophy-winning quarterbacks Angelo Bertelli and Johnny Lujack on the football field, but the vivacious runner stood right at the front of the line when it came to those who starred for Notre Dame coach Frank Leahy.

"If he'd been born 25 years later, he'd be worth at least $500,000 a year with an NFL team," raved Leahy, who called the son of early-1900s Irish star Harry "Red" Miller the greatest back he ever coached.

Miller led the nation with 911 rushing yards but finished fourth in the Heisman Trophy balloting during the 1943 season. The Cleveland native chose a career in law over pro football but was instrumental in forming what became the powerful NFL Players' Association.

Creighton Miller, a reserve fullback and the last in a family of Notre Dame standouts, runs with the ball in a 16–0 win over Carnegie Tech in 1941.

or that the sophomore who stepped in to take his place would claim one of his own before he graduated.

Johnny Lujack took over for Bertelli and quarterbacked the Irish to romps over Army (26–0) and Northwestern (25–6) and a 14–13 nail-biter against Iowa Pre-Flight, a U.S. Navy-commissioned school that emphasized football as a means of training. Great Lakes, an Illinois-based naval training school, ruined Notre Dame's perfect season when it scored with 33 seconds remaining for a 19–14 win in the finale. Still, with a record of 9–1, the Fighting Irish were the unanimous choice as national champion.

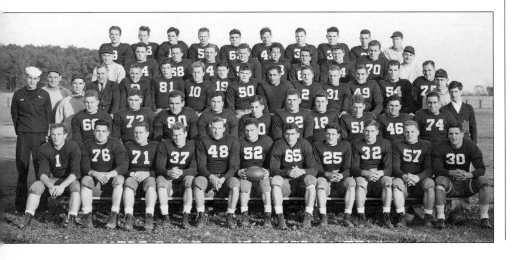

1943 Heisman Trophy Winner Angelo Bertelli

Angelo Bertelli, who Coach Frank Leahy once called "the finest passer and the worst runner" he'd ever coached, carries the ball in this 1941 victory over Arizona. Two years later, Bertelli ran away with the Heisman Trophy.

Legendary sportswriter Grantland Rice called him "the T-formation magician." And like any good magician, Angelo Bertelli knew that "practice, practice, practice" was the recipe for perfect performance. When Coach Frank Leahy told the Massachusetts native before the 1942 season that Notre Dame would be switching to the T-formation, Bertelli estimated he took "a thousand snaps, maybe a million," in preparation that summer.

In 1941, Bertelli, as a single-wing halfback, led the nation with almost 57 percent of his tosses completed. "Bert," Leahy told him, "you're the finest passer and the worst runner I've ever coached." The switch to the T would make the best use of Bertelli's strong and accurate right arm, while leaving the running to his more capable teammates.

There were some growing pains when Bertelli first took snaps directly from the center's rump in 1942. When the Fighting Irish lost two games and tied two others, fans were quick to question Leahy's decision to abandon the attack favored by his mentor, Knute Rockne. The 1943 season was shaping up to be a critical one for Leahy and Bertelli. They came through in magical fashion.

Bertelli was brilliant, though he played just six games before the Marine Corps activated him for service in World War II. He completed 25 of 36 passes, including ten for touchdowns. Under his direction, Notre Dame pummeled Pittsburgh, Georgia Tech, Michigan, Wisconsin, Illinois, and Navy by an average score of 44–5.

Bertelli, a football, baseball, and hockey star in high school, had finished second in the Heisman Trophy balloting in 1941 and sixth in 1942. Despite playing only half of the 1943 season, he ran away with the honor. The Notre Dame quarterback's 648 points were nearly four times as many as runner-up Bob O'Dell from Penn.

Even higher honors were still to come. Bertelli served as a captain in the marines, earning a Bronze Star and a Purple Heart in World War II. He completed his degree upon returning from the war, played professionally for Chicago and Los Angeles of the All-American Football Conference, and became a successful New Jersey businessman.

Before his death at age 78, Bertelli also became involved in youth football programs in New Jersey. Notre Damers Nick Buoniconti and Joe Scibelli were among the products of his mentoring.

1946: Notre Dame 0, Army 0

After the 1943 national championship season, Leahy (left) served in the navy for two years during World War II. He rejoined the Irish as head coach in 1946.

Something about the Notre Dame–Army rivalry fascinated football fans in the early 20th century. The series seemed to have everything: eastern power vs. western power; the "Win One for The Gipper" game; beloved Catholic school vs. Armed Forces training ground. In 1946, the game had one other theme: revenge.

Army had shut out Notre Dame by scores of 59–0 and 48–0 the previous two seasons, while Coach Frank Leahy was serving in World War II. Now that Leahy was back on the sideline and his team was back in form, having routed its first five opponents, all eyes were on Yankee Stadium for a November 9 battle. "Certainly, this football game has won the fancy of the gridiron intelligentsia and has assumed mammoth proportions like a heavyweight championship bout," reported *The New York Times.*

Army had won 25 straight games. Leahy, who often downplayed his team's chances in hopes of gaining an edge, went one step further before this game, predicting Army would win by a 27–14 score behind the experience and speed of Doc Blanchard ("Mr. Inside") and Glenn Davis ("Mr. Outside"). More than 74,000 fans expected an offensive showcase.

Instead, they got a scoreless tie. Leahy wound up 41 points off in his assessment. The Irish were quick to tie up Davis and Blanchard every time they touched the ball. The one time Blanchard found daylight, Notre Dame's Johnny Lujack, who played both offense and defense, raced over for a head-on tackle 36 yards short of the goal line. It was the end of Army's best threat.

Notre Dame compiled 173 yards to Army's 138. The Irish marched 85 yards in the second quarter—easily the best drive of the game—but the Cadet defense made a stand with the visitors just three yards from the goal line.

Lujack, Davis, and Blanchard were among the players who logged a full 60 minutes in the game. But by the final gun, both teams were drained, scoreless, and still unbeaten.

Notre Dame halfback Bill Gompers makes his way to Army's five-yard line during the famed 1946 scoreless tie between the national powers at Yankee Stadium.

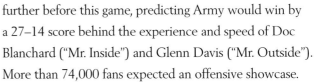

Leahy's Two-Year Absence

For the Fighting Irish, the 1944 and 1945 seasons were strange ones, indeed. The school needed a football coach when Frank Leahy joined the navy following the national title season of 1943. It turned to Ed McKeever, a Leahy assistant who inherited a team depleted by graduation and military assignments.

The Irish went 8–2, but back-to-back losses to Navy (32–13) and Army (59–0) were telling. McKeever took the head-coaching job at Cornell after the 1944 season.

Enter Hugh Devore, a 1934 Notre Dame graduate and another Leahy aide who had head-coaching experience at Providence and the College of the Holy Cross in Massachusetts. He guided Notre Dame to a 7–2–1 mark in 1945, with a 48–0 loss to Army and 39–7 loss to Great Lakes on his ledger.

Nevertheless, Fighting Irish fans were thrilled to welcome back Leahy. He signed a ten-year contract after his discharge from the navy, introduced himself to a group of players who had never met him, and celebrated his return by directing Notre Dame to four consecutive undefeated seasons.

1947 Heisman Trophy Winner Johnny Lujack

Great quarterbacks do not grow on trees, as any coach will tell you. They do, for whatever reason, grow up in western Pennsylvania. Johnny Unitas, George Blanda, Joe Namath, Jim Kelly, Dan Marino, and Joe Montana are among those who hail from this blue-collar area of the country, where toughness is demanded and football is king.

Preceding them all was the pride of Connellsville, a small town southeast of Pittsburgh. Johnny Lujack, the youngest of four boys, starred in everything he tried in high school. Blessed with wholesome good looks that could have earned movie roles in Hollywood and an arm that both baseball and football teams would covet, he turned down an appointment to the U.S. Military Academy at West Point and dozens of scholarship offers to fulfill a lifelong dream. "Notre Dame was a magical word for me," Lujack said.

In those days, it was rare for a sophomore even to make the varsity. But in 1943, Lujack not only made the Fighting Irish as a second-year man, he also wound up playing a leading role when quarterback Angelo Bertelli left for World War II midseason.

In his first game, before 75,000-plus fans at Yankee Stadium, he passed for two touchdowns and ran for another to lead the undefeated Irish to a 26–0 win over Army. He was an instant celebrity. Though Bertelli won the Heisman Trophy for his early efforts, it was Lujack who preserved the run to Frank Leahy's first national title as coach.

After missing the '44 and '45 seasons while serving in the navy, Lujack returned to South Bend and made some of Notre Dame's greatest plays—on both sides of scrimmage—during the undefeated seasons of 1946 and 1947.

In a memorable battle against Army in 1946, it was Lujack's bone-jarring tackle of Doc Blanchard that saved a touchdown, preserving a scoreless tie and allowing Notre Dame to secure another national championship.

Then, in 1947, Lujack became Notre Dame's second Heisman Trophy winner when his passing, defense, and kicking led the Irish to nine straight wins by a combined 291–52 margin. He completed 56 percent of his passes, including nine for touchdowns, and beat out New York Yankees star Joe DiMaggio for the Associated Press Male Athlete of the Year Award before embarking on a brief but successful career as a quarterback for the Chicago Bears.

A western Pennsylvania tradition was born.

His looks said Hollywood, but his skills said end zone. Johnny Lujack was an exceptional athlete who quarterbacked, defended, and kicked Notre Dame to a remarkable run of success en route to the 1947 Heisman Trophy.

NOTRE DAME
"Fighting Irish"

PITTSBURGH 40-6
PURDUE 22-7
NEBRASKA 31-0
IOWA 21-0
SO. CALIFORNIA 38-7

UNDEFEATED 1947 UNTIED

NAVY 27-0
ARMY 27-7
NORTHWESTERN 26-19
TULANE 59-6

National Champions

Only one foe—Northwestern—managed to score more than a touchdown against Notre Dame's 1947 powerhouse.

National Champions
NOTRE DAME 1949

The 1949 Fighting Irish outscored their opponents by a 360–86 margin en route to ten convincing wins and a national title.

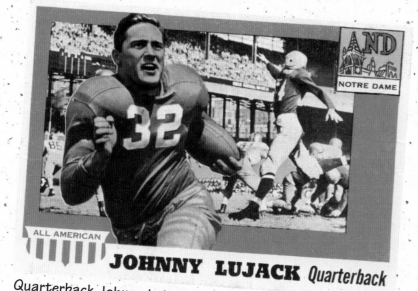

AND
NOTRE DAME

ALL AMERICAN
JOHNNY LUJACK Quarterback

Quarterback Johnny Lujack was a consensus All-American in 1946 and 1947. He finished third in the Heisman Trophy race in 1946 and won it in '47.

Football cleats bore a striking resemblance to work boots in the 1940s and '50s, and the Fighting Irish went to work with great success.

Notre Dame's star-studded 1947 national champs needed no introduction around the South Bend campus. Their names were also well known to opponents.

NOTRE DAME

1943

FILLEY (CAPT) COLEMAN PERKO

LIMONT WHITE CZAROBSKI YONAKOR

MILLER MELLO LUJACK RYKOVICH

NATIONAL CHAMPIONS

Pat Filley captained the 1943 Fighting Irish to nine wins in ten games and a national championship with help from the likes of Creighton Miller, Johnny Lujack, and others.

This 1950s-era pennant withstood the elements and represented several more successful seasons in Fighting Irish history.

Moose Takes Over Irish Athletics

A young Moose Krause made a name for himself as Notre Dame's basketball coach before taking the entire athletic department to new heights.

oaching Notre Dame's football team has never been a 40-hour-a-week job. With his team in the midst of a 39-game unbeaten streak after World War II, that became abundantly clear to Frank Leahy. He had been heading the athletic department since his arrival as coach in 1941, but his workdays during the fall could last 16 to 18 hours. It would be "prudent for the University," he said in 1949, to turn over the athletic director responsibilities to someone else.

Notre Dame did not have to look far to find the perfect man for the job. It turned to its very own Moose.

Edward W. "Moose" Krause was Notre Dame's basketball coach when he accepted the athletic director position in March 1949. Now he would face the task of handling two jobs simultaneously at a time when college sports were growing rapidly. If there was ever a person up to the task, it was Moose, a big, broad-grinning, cigar-smoking man who won All-American honors in basketball and football at Notre Dame and graduated with a journalism degree in 1934.

Some called Krause "Saint Edward." Others called him "Mr. Notre Dame." Long-time Notre Dame president Father Theodore Hesburgh described him as the "Rock of Gibraltar, the soul of integrity."

Krause was many things to many people: World War II hero, Alcoholics Anonymous spokesperson, devoted husband and father. As leader of Notre Dame's athletic department for more than three decades, the Chicago native took great pride not only in the success of the football, basketball, and other varsity teams but in the establishment of a strong intramural program that allowed all students to get involved in sports.

The 6'3" Krause, basketball's second three-time All-American, was so dominant as a post player that the NCAA instituted the three-second rule, an idea designed, in large part, to keep him out of the lane. Though basketball was his first love, in 1951 he fired himself as hoops coach. "Best move I ever made," he said. "We needed a change." He was then able to focus exclusively on making Notre Dame's athletic department the best it could be.

By the time Krause retired in 1980, Notre Dame had added women's varsity programs, boasted the best intramural football program in the country, and retained its national presence in varsity football and basketball. Krause died in 1992 at age 79.

Moose Krause cared for Notre Dame athletics in much the same way he cared for his wife, Elise. Father Theodore Hesburgh said of Krause, "If I ever met a saint, he was one of them."

1949 Heisman Trophy Winner Leon Hart

A lineman as Heisman Trophy winner? Why not? If games are won and lost in the trenches—and indeed they are—then it should make perfect sense for a dominant lineman to be honored as the country's most outstanding college football player. But historically, there have been two obstacles to such a scenario. First, linemen do the dirty work: blocking, creating holes, and tying up opponents so their teammates can make the headlines. Second, linemen rarely compile statistics that would allow for comparison. Traditionally, they toil in obscurity.

But Leon Hart was no ordinary lineman. In 1949, the three-time first-team All-American became the second lineman ever to win the Heisman Trophy, and he remains the last lineman to claim the honor.

Those who watched him play did not consider his award a stretch at all. For starters, Hart *did* have statistics. The two-way end, a four-year monogram winner, was a talented pass catcher. He hauled in 16 receptions as a junior and 19 as a senior, catching 13 touchdown passes in his career. He was also a terror on end-around carries, nimble enough to elude would-be tacklers and strong enough, at 6'4" and 245 pounds, to run right through them. When the Irish needed a critical yard, it was not uncommon to see Hart line up at fullback. As a defensive end, Hart was a force opposing coaches would alter their game plans to avoid.

Above all else, Hart was a class act. During his freshman year, when someone posted a sign giving the name of a student who would accept wagers, he tore it to shreds and shouted, "This has no place in a Notre Dame locker room!"

Playing both offense and defense, Hart was a two-way starter who never experienced a loss in his Notre Dame career. He led the Fighting Irish to a 36–0–2 record and three national championships. In addition to winning the Heisman Trophy in 1949, he also took the Maxwell Award as Player of the Year and beat out the likes of Jackie Robinson and Sam Snead as Associated Press Male Athlete of the Year.

The Pennsylvania native earned a degree in mechanical engineering, but before hanging up his cleats, he led the Detroit Lions to three NFL titles during his eight pro seasons. In 1951, Hart was the last player selected All-Pro on both offense and defense.

As a 17-year-old freshman in 1946, Leon Hart was the youngest member of Notre Dame's national championship team. He was also named first-team All-American as a sophomore.

A Heisman-to-Heisman connection saw Hart catch a pass from Johnny Lujack during Notre Dame's 27–7 win over Army in 1947.

The Streak

The years from 1946 to 1950 were not always the most content in Frank Leahy's life. Winning can earn you enemies. And for 39 consecutive games, a stretch of more than four full seasons, Leahy's Fighting Irish were unstoppable. A scoreless tie against Army in 1946 and a 14–14 stalemate with Southern Cal in the final game of 1948 were the only blemishes during a span that featured a 21-game winning streak and three national championships.

One of the greatest dynasties in college football history did not come without controversy. Some accused Leahy of playing dirty. Certainly, his teams blocked harder and tackled more surely than any in the land. They were relentless. Army dropped Notre Dame from its slate after a 27–7 loss to the Fighting Irish in 1947. Other schools would not schedule "Leahy's Lads" in the first place. There were whispers even from within Notre Dame's administration that perhaps the program was becoming *too* powerful.

"The reason they complain," former Illinois legend Red Grange once said, "is that Leahy is superior and he wins. [Other schools] stay clear of Notre Dame for one reason. They don't want to get beat."

In the years following World War II, Leahy and several veterans, some of whom had been regulars on the 1942 and 1943 Irish squads, were back in the fold. Leahy had certainly added to his depth by recruiting some players while in the navy. The talent that donned the blue and gold—names like Johnny Lujack, Leon Hart, Frank Tripucka, Bill Fischer, Emil Sitko, and Bob Williams—was remarkable. It was no wonder Notre Dame began selling out every home game.

Most opponents did not stand a chance against Notre Dame's juggernaut. The 1946 team outscored its foes 271–24, shutting out opponents five times and never allowing more than six points in a game en route to a national title. The Irish defended their championship the following fall, winning nine straight games by a cumulative 291–52 score. During the 39-game unbeaten run, Notre Dame tallied 1,256 points to its opponents' 262—an average margin of 32–7.

With Tripucka taking over the quarterback duties from the great, Heisman Trophy-winning Lujack in 1948, Notre Dame did escape some close calls. Its streak nearly came to an end in the 1948 season opener against Purdue when Steve Oracko's 25-yard field goal in the waning minutes produced a 28–27 win. "They probably used up a season's

A rainy, 29–19 victory at Northwestern brought the Irish winning streak to 15 games. Notre Dame ended the 1947 season 9–0–0.

The Irish eked out a 28–27 home victory over Purdue in the 1948 season opener, keeping alive an unbeaten streak that included a classic scoreless tie with Army in 1946.

The top-ranked Fighting Irish routed No. 17 Southern Cal 32–0 on their way to a 10–0–0 ledger in 1949.

The Greatest Team Ever?

Bill Furlong, former *Newsweek* sports editor and *Chicago Daily News* columnist, compared the 1947 Notre Dame Fighting Irish to a pro franchise. Eighteen years after winning the national title, he called it the greatest college team of all time, "grinding its way to immortality as a glacier grinds towards eternity: crushingly, relentlessly."

Now, more than 60 years after drubbing their nine opponents by an average score of 32–7, the 1947 Fighting Irish still merit mention as one of the best—if not *the* best—ever. More than 40 members of the squad made it to the pros. The team featured not one, but two Heisman Trophy winners: senior quarterback Johnny Lujack (1947) and sophomore lineman Leon Hart (1949). Referring to the 1947 Fighting Irish squad, former quarterback George Ratterman said, "There's no question in my mind that Notre Dame would have beaten any team in professional football except the Cleveland Browns."

How good were the Irish? Facing Southern Cal in a season-ending battle of unbeatens to determine the national title, Notre Dame stunned its opponents—and a crowd of nearly 105,000 at the Los Angeles Memorial Coliseum—by a 38–7 score. It was no contest.

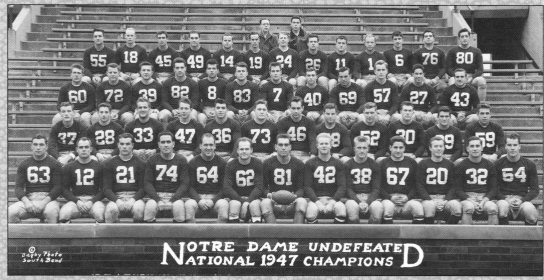

Notre Dame's undefeated 1947 national championship team boasted five All-Americans, including that year's Heisman Trophy winner, Johnny Lujack (32), and 1949 Heisman winner Leon Hart (82).

quota of luck," Luke Carroll of the *New York Herald Tribune* wrote of the Irish victory.

In another close call in 1948, Notre Dame trailed Northwestern entering the fourth quarter until Billy Gay's late touchdown salvaged a 12–7 triumph, and a touchdown and extra point in the final minute were required to secure the 14–all deadlock with USC in the season finale. The tie wound up costing Notre Dame a third straight national championship, but the Irish roared back in 1949 to win all ten games impressively for a third title in four years.

But on October 7, 1950, Notre Dame finally met its match. As Leahy had predicted before the contest, his graduation-depleted team lost for the first time in 40 games, by a 28–14 score against visiting Purdue. It was the first of four losses that season.

Leahy was tired. Those who knew him could see it. The pressure of such high expectations, and perhaps some of the outside criticism, had taken a toll. Leahy did what came naturally. He went back to work toward his next national title. And his players followed his lead. "We work hard," he noted. "We try not to miss any possibilities."

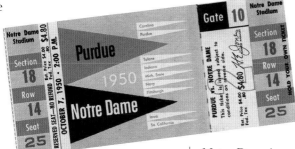

Notre Dame's 39-game unbeaten streak finally came to an end in 1950, when Purdue scored a 28–14 upset in the rain in South Bend.

Paul Hornung's 1956 Heisman was the fifth such trophy won by a Notre Dame player.

If at first it doesn't rhyme, try try again. Joe Theismann, after a famous pronunciation change, finished second to Jim Plunkett in the 1970 Heisman race.

THEISMANN FOR HEISMAN

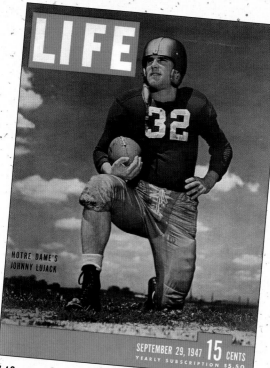

LIFE

NOTRE DAME'S JOHNNY LUJACK

SEPTEMBER 29, 1947   15 CENTS
YEARLY SUBSCRIPTION $5.50

Life magazine honored Notre Dame quarterback Johnny Lujack with a cover in 1947, his Heisman-winning season.

All seven Notre Dame Heisman Trophy winners signed this commemorative football.

NOTRE DAME HEISMAN WINNERS

Leon Hart
LEON HART
1949

John Huarte
JOHN HUARTE
1964

Angelo Bertelli
ANGELO BERTELLI
1943

Johnny Lattner
JOHN LATTNER
1953

Paul Hornung
PAUL HORNUNG
1956

Tim Brown
TIM BROWN
1987

John Lujack
JOHN LUJACK
1947

Special Edition
3621 of 5000

An all-purpose standout, Johnny Lattner (14) looks to make a block during Notre Dame's 1953 victory over Georgia Tech.

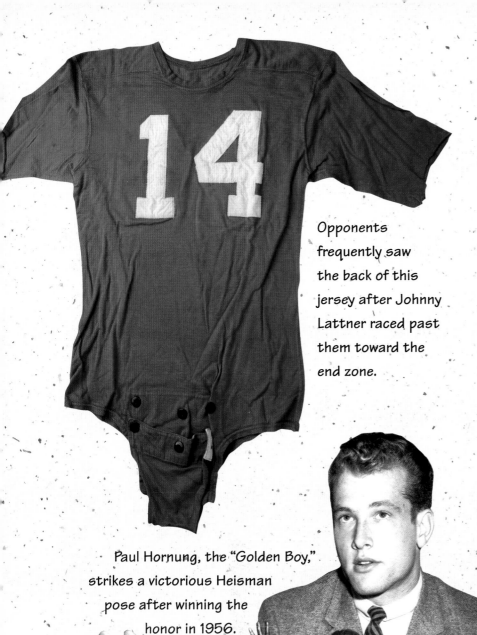

Opponents frequently saw the back of this jersey after Johnny Lattner raced past them toward the end zone.

Paul Hornung, the "Golden Boy," strikes a victorious Heisman pose after winning the honor in 1956.

Heisman Trophy Leaders

Notre Dame's seven Heisman trophies ties it with Southern Cal and Ohio State for the most by a single school. Here's a breakdown of those winners, and a list of other schools with multiple winners.

Notre Dame	Ohio State	Southern California
Angelo Bertelli (1943)	Les Horvath (1944)	Mike Garrett (1965)
Johnny Lujack (1947)	Vic Janowicz (1950)	O. J. Simpson (1968)
Leon Hart (1949)	Howard Cassady (1955)	Charles White (1979)
Johnny Lattner (1953)	Archie Griffin (1974 & 1975)	Marcus Allen (1981)
Paul Hornung (1956)		Carson Palmer (2002)
John Huarte (1964)	Eddie George (1995)	Matt Leinart (2004)
Tim Brown (1987)	Troy Smith (2006)	Reggie Bush (2005)

Other schools with multiple winners: Oklahoma—4; Army, Florida, Michigan, Nebraska—3; Auburn, Florida State, Georgia, Miami, Navy, Texas, Wisconsin, Yale—2

Notre Dame's seven Heisman Trophy winners (from left): Johnny Lujack, Angelo Bertelli, Leon Hart, Tim Brown, Paul Hornung, John Huarte, and Johnny Lattner.

First ND Game on TV: 1952 Upset of Oklahoma

Young fans of television and college football might be surprised to learn that the two did not always go hand in hand. The first televised game, between Fordham and Waynesburg in 1939, did get other colleges curious about featuring their own games on the air. In 1950, Penn and Notre Dame arranged contracts with separate TV networks to broadcast their games. Penn's home dates were aired on ABC that season. Notre Dame's were to be shown on the DuMont Network beginning in 1951.

However, the NCAA had other plans. Fearing that fans would begin staying home to watch football on TV rather than buying tickets to the games, it nullified Penn's and Notre Dame's contracts for 1951—before a Fighting Irish game ever reached the tube. It softened its stance before the 1952 campaign but insisted on limiting the telecasts to one per week and controlling which games would be shown.

So it was that the Fighting Irish had to wait until November 8, 1952, to play a televised game. Those who witnessed the thriller, whether they watched at Notre Dame Stadium or from living room sofas across the country, would attest that it was worth the wait from an Irish perspective.

Oklahoma entered the game undefeated, ranked fourth, and a two-touchdown favorite. Halfback Billy Vessels, en route to the Heisman Trophy that season, scored all three Sooner touchdowns on sprints of 62 and 42 yards and a 28-yard reception, as the visitors amassed leads of 7–0, 14–7, and 21–14. Vessels carried 17 times for 195 yards.

Thanks largely to six turnovers, however, the Sooners were limited to half of their 42-point scoring average. After Notre Dame tied the score 21–21 early in the fourth quarter, the game turned on a helmet-jarring collision. Larry Grigg fielded Notre Dame's ensuing kickoff and began racing upfield. After 20 yards, a locomotivelike linebacker named Dan Shannon met him at full speed, dislodging the football on a hit that could be heard from inside the press box high above the field. "It was like two freight trains coming together," Notre Dame's Johnny Lattner recalled. Both Grigg and Shannon had to be helped off the field after Notre Dame's Al Kohanowich fell on the fumble.

A 17-yard carry by Lattner set up Tom Carey for the game-winning touchdown on a quarterback sneak. The final score: Notre Dame 27, Oklahoma 21. And it said so right there on national television.

Moving pictures changed the face of college football for fans across the country. For the Fighting Irish faithful, it began with a 1952 upset of Oklahoma and included closed-circuit broadcasts in several big-city hotels.

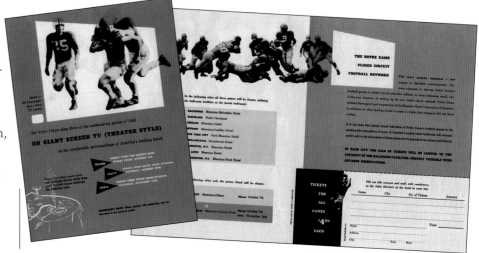

Game Day

merican families began stockpiling two cars per family in the prosperous days following World War II. Judging by the slow parade of traffic crawling toward Notre Dame Stadium on football Saturdays, it seemed a good percentage of those vehicles belonged to fans of the Fighting Irish, who enjoyed loading up the trunks with pregame food, beverages, and perhaps a blanket or two to stave off the brisk, northern Indiana wind.

It was also during the postwar era that home crowds of 50,000-plus became standard at "the house that Rockne built." But those fans would not save their Sunday best for Sundays.

"People were dressed up," recalled Washington State football coach Bill Doba, a South Bend native who vividly

remembers cheering the Fighting Irish as a youth. "Women were in hose and heels and furs and men were in sport coats. It was like going to church. There was a reverence about it."

Reverend Robert Angelle, who still follows Irish football with the same passion he had as a student in the 1950s, describes the scene from a half-century ago:

"As classes wound down for the week, the students finished decorating the outside of their dorms with banners promoting the invincibility of the Irish," he said. "As dusk approached, the Notre Dame band became pied pipers, circling campus and enticing students to follow to the Fieldhouse for the pep rally.

"On Saturday, a beautiful scene unfolded. Visitors toured the campus, led by organized guides. Families had picnics on blankets. Nothing elaborate. The focus was just being there and enjoying the camaraderie."

The Irish made their television debut in 1952, and the following year a deal with Box Office Television, Inc., was announced that would allow Notre Dame football to be shown in certain movie theaters across the country.

Whether during the glory days of Leahy in the 1940s and early 1950s or the struggles of Terry Brennan and Joe Kuharich in the late 1950s and early 1960s, the Fighting Irish retained a national following that no program could match. In the fall, it was not unusual for parochial school priests and nuns to lead their classes in Friday prayers that asked for a Notre Dame victory… God willing, of course.

Student publication Scholastic *documented this scene on a 1950 cover. Notre Dame crowds from this dominant era were well dressed and ready to celebrate another Fighting Irish victory.*

The Class that Knew No Loss

Each summer, the University of Notre Dame holds its class reunions in five-year intervals. That means everyone who graduated in a year ending in "0" or "5" can gather in subsequent years ending in "0" and "5" to toast their days on campus, compare family photos, and catch up with old friends.

Those "0" and "5" classes also get the chance to meet members of the Class of 1950 and tell them how lucky they were. When it comes to football, they were "The Class." The class without a loss. The class with three national titles.

Leon Hart, 1949 Heisman Trophy winner, was president of the Class of 1950. He and about a dozen others were four-year players who posted a 36–0–2 record. The closest a Notre Dame student who enrolled in 1946 and graduated four years later came to witnessing a defeat were ties with Army in 1946 and Southern Cal in 1948. Both of those games were on the road. How very lucky indeed.

Students from the Class of 1950 never saw a loss.

1953 Heisman Trophy Winner Johnny Lattner

Little Johnny Lattner was just nine years old when he drove his father's truck for the first time. He called it the greatest thrill of his life, at least until he steered the vehicle through the window of a neighborhood butcher store on Chicago's west side. Years later, opposing football players would not have much better luck trying to stop Lattner, Notre Dame's fourth Heisman Trophy winner.

Lattner could have attended any college of his choice on a scholarship after a high school career in which he starred in every sport he played and made all-state at two different football positions: end and halfback. But one trip to South

There was little Lattner could not do, including flying toward the camera for the cover of the 1952 Notre Dame football guide.

Bend was all the convincing Lattner needed. "I saw that golden dome with the statue of our Blessed Mother all [lit] up," he recalled. "I got kind of choked up."

Lattner arrived a few years after most college football players had chosen either offense or defense, but not both—not that it mattered in his case. He was fast, athletic, aggressive, and smart. He could run, defend, and return kicks with the best of them. His all-around skills made it difficult for Coach Frank Leahy to yank him off the field, so it was not unusual for Lattner to play all 60 minutes. Opposing coaches would have preferred he take a few plays off. "He's a great boy," noted Michigan State's Clarence "Biggie" Munn, "and one murderous runner to put up with."

A regular at halfback and in the defensive secondary for three years (1951–53), Lattner was the first player to win back-to-back Maxwell awards as College Player of the Year (1952 and 1953). He set school records on offense, defense, and special teams. He intercepted 13 career passes, returned two kickoffs for scores as a senior, and put an all-purpose yardage mark in the books that stood until Vagas Ferguson broke it in 1979.

Lattner carried Notre Dame to a 9–0–1 record in 1953, when several sources (not including the AP or UPI polls) awarded the Fighting Irish the national championship. And although he did not lead the team in rushing, passing, receiving, or scoring, his all-around excellence earned him the Heisman Trophy over Minnesota's Paul Giel by a narrow 56 points in the balloting. It remains one of the closest Heisman Trophy races in the history of the award.

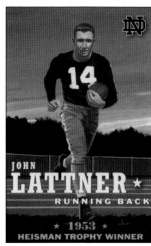

One of the closest Heisman Trophy races in history saw the multi-talented Johnny Lattner edge Minnesota's Paul Giel to become Notre Dame's fourth winner of the coveted award.

The Terry Brennan Years

Terry Brennan wore not a wrinkle on his face or a gray hair on his head when he was named Frank Leahy's successor in 1954. He was 25, so young that even his mother wondered about the hire. "In this job," he noted to reporters, "I'll age fast."

Brennan had played for Leahy, rushing for 1,269 career yards before graduating in 1949. He coached Chicago's Mount Carmel High School to great success before returning to guide Notre Dame's freshman squad in 1953. He took the head post the following year, when Leahy's doctors insisted that he step down. The year before, Leahy had been stricken with acute pancreatitis and had been given last rites. Leahy's career record was 87–11–9.

Brennan did not seem too concerned about the shoes he had to fill. He would be 26 before the start of the '54 season, he quipped, and he had halfback Joe Heap and quarterback Ralph Guglielmi returning, along with a terrific group of sophomores that included Paul Hornung.

Brennan opened his career with a 21–0 rout of Texas, as the Fighting Irish ascended to a top national ranking. Although they lost that spot with a 27–14 defeat at the hands of Purdue the following week, Notre Dame finished the season with eight straight wins for a 9–1 ledger. Brennan's team went 8–2 in 1955, falling to Michigan State and Southern Cal.

If the young coach had not yet experienced the rapid aging process that comes from coaching college football, he certainly did in 1956. Despite Hornung's all-around excellence, a graduation-depleted Fighting Irish team took a dramatic dive. Notre Dame finished 2–8, its worst record ever, sending pundits scrambling to blame scholarship limitations, a de-emphasis on football, and, of course, the "greenhorn" running the program.

Better-experienced troops helped Brennan rebound with 7–3 and 6–4 seasons in 1957 and 1958, but it was not enough to save his job. He was fired at the ripe old age of 30.

Irish End Sooners's Record Streak

What Notre Dame was to college football in the 1940s, Oklahoma became in the 1950s. Bud Wilkinson's powerhouse Sooners steamrolled anyone in their path. Entering a November 16, 1957, game against Notre Dame before 63,000 home fans, the Sooners were riding a record 47-game winning streak and were 18-point favorites. Many expected they would prevail by much more against an Irish team that had gone 2–8 during the previous season, including a 40–0 embarrassment at the hands of the Sooners.

"Games of the Century" are numerous in college football. For Notre Dame, this was one of them. The Irish ascended not only to the level of their opponent, but above it. Notre Dame's defense was a brick wall against the Sooners's powerful attack, forcing a scoreless tie into the fourth quarter.

Then, in the closing minutes, Bob Williams's throws, Nick Pietrosante's smashing runs, and a three-yard touchdown sweep by Dick Lynch on fourth down with 3:50 to play clinched one of the greatest upsets in college football history. It was the first time the Sooners failed to score in 123 contests.

Dick Lynch goes in for the game's only touchdown in the fourth quarter of Notre Dame's stunning 7–0 upset of Oklahoma in 1957.

Terry Brennan played halfback for three national title teams under Frank Leahy. He returned to his alma mater to coach, eventually taking over the head position vacated by Leahy in 1954.

The South Bend Tribune documented Notre Dame's shocking upset of Oklahoma in 1957.

Meanwhile, *The Daily Oklahoman* recounted the loss for stunned Sooners fans, who saw their team's 47-game winning streak halted.

Coaches Frank Leahy (left) and Elmer Layden don't seem to mind the cold weather of 1941, nor does mascot Clashmore Mike during a dominant era in Irish football.

The Notre Dame–Michigan State rivalry began in 1897, and the Megaphone Trophy has been awarded to the winner each year since 1949.

In the 1940s and '50s, ads for Keds sneakers boasted: "You'll get speed and sports enjoyment in every pair of Frank Leahy Keds. Treat yourself to them soon!"

Frank Leahy was named college football's Coach of the Year in 1941 after going undefeated in his first year as Irish head coach.

COACH FRANK LEAHY SAYS,

"WIN IN KEDS!"

"In any fast game and for all sports, you'll do better for your team, and have more fun, if you wear correct athletic shoes. I was happy to advise on the design of new Frank Leahy Keds, so that your footwork can help you get the most from healthful, manly sports."

—FRANK LEAHY

Here's how Frank Leahy told us to build the new Keds named for him:

★ *Rugged construction;* note those burly, non-slip, ground-grip soles.

★ *Cool, light uppers* that "breathe" when you move — they're washable.

★ *Speed built in* — note the no-bind, slant-cut tops, the lace-to-toe design that braces arch and ankle, and the special arch-supporting straps.

★ *Scientific construction for stamina* — the *Shockproof Arch Cushion* and *Cushioned Insole* give you resilient footing, so legs and feet don't soon get tired. You'll enjoy staying in the game longer.

Yes, you'll get speed and sports enjoyment in every pair of Frank Leahy Keds. Treat yourself to them soon!

Ask your store for FREE 48-page Keds Handbook of Sports and Games.

Natural *Support!*

KEDS SHOCKPROOF ARCH CUSHION AND SCIENTIFIC LAST

Cushioned Insole

Shockproof Arch Cushion and Cushioned Heel

Scientific Last For Straight-Line Toe-Action

u.s. **Keds**®

The Shoe of Champions

UNITED STATES RUBBER COMPANY

Rockefeller Center, New York

Father Joyce

The man involved in every major athletics decision at Notre Dame for 35 years was warming up his pitching arm at the Loftus Sports Center after his 1987 retirement as executive vice president of the university. As usual, Father Edmund P. Joyce had a partner in the bullpen session by the name of Father Theodore Hesburgh, who had stepped down from his post as Notre Dame's president at the same time.

The priests were preparing for a 1989 cross-country road trip in an RV, and one of their stops involved throwing out ceremonial first pitches before a baseball game at Yankee Stadium. As usual, "Ned" Joyce left nothing to chance.

It was that way throughout his tenure as Hesburgh's right-hand man from 1952 to 1987, a period in which Joyce grew Notre Dame athletics into a multimillion-dollar department featuring more than two dozen men's and women's programs.

Televised football was in its infancy when Joyce, a 1937 Notre Dame graduate who was ordained 12 years later, took his administrative post. He was a driving force in the push for TV exposure for the sport, and Notre Dame profited handsomely from his efforts. The university's endowment under Joyce and Hesburgh grew from $9 million to more than $400 million, with athletic revenues playing no small role.

More impressive than the dollars were the standards under which Joyce shepherded the Fighting Irish programs. He once told a *Sports Illustrated* reporter that the magazine had carte-blanche access to Irish athletics any time they wanted to do a story. "That's how strongly he

Edmund P. Joyce was Theodore Hesburgh's right-hand man for 35 years. When it came to Notre Dame athletics, however, Father Ned was front and center.

felt that ND's athletic program was beyond reproach," said John Heisler, senior associate athletic director.

Admissions standards were set high for Notre Dame recruits, even under growing pressure to win. Joyce was a College Football Association and NCAA spokesperson for keeping the "student" first in "student-athlete."

"I've never known anybody in my life who was as wonderful a person as Ned Joyce," Hesburgh said in eulogizing Joyce, who died in 2004 at age 87.

Father Ted

During their 35-year tenure as Notre Dame president and vice president, respectively, it was said that Father Hesburgh was the man with the books and Father Joyce was the man with the tickets. It was more complicated than that, of course, but the division of labor worked beautifully for academic and athletic growth.

From 1952 to 1987, under Theodore Hesburgh's tutelage, Notre Dame's enrollment more than doubled to 9,676 undergraduates. When he started, 30 percent of those students ranked in the top 10 percent of their high school classes. It was 95 percent when he retired.

Hesburgh, like Joyce, was a sports fan who took pride in Notre Dame's championships. Though Joyce did more than perhaps anyone but Knute Rockne in leading Notre Dame football to the forefront, Hesburgh might well be called the "Rock" of school leadership. "If you ask American college presidents who is the most successful [college] president they know," said Georgetown president Timothy Healy in 1987, "they'll say, 'Ted Hesburgh.'"

Father Theodore Hesburgh is the recipient of 150 honorary degrees and the Presidential Medal of Freedom.

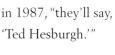

Father Hesburgh presents his friend Pope Paul VI (left) with an honorary degree from the University of Notre Dame on June 1, 1960.

A longtime champion for civil rights, Father Hesburgh (second from left) joins hands with Dr. Martin Luther King, Jr., during a demonstration in Chicago in 1964.

The Golden Boy:
1956 Heisman Trophy Winner Paul Hornung

There has been only one player to win the Heisman Trophy on a team with a losing record. Then again, there has been only one Paul Hornung. Ed Sullivan, Notre Dame's center in 1956, said the Fighting Irish ran only one play that season. "I'd hike the ball to Paul [Hornung]," he recalled, "and we'd all just get the hell out of the way."

Hornung became known as Notre Dame's "Golden Boy." He stood out off the field for his blond hair, boyish good looks, and affable personality. The Louisville native never met a one-liner he didn't like—or at least try. On the field, he was every bit as striking for his proficiency as a passer, runner, and kicker.

"Paul Hornung," said Notre Dame coach Frank Leahy, who recruited him away from Kentucky, Indiana, Purdue, Miami, and Florida, among others, "will be the greatest quarterback Notre Dame ever had. He runs like a mower going through grass. Tackles just fall off him."

Leahy retired before the 1954 season, when Hornung became eligible for the varsity. Under Terry Brennan, the sophomore averaged 6.9 yards per carry as a backup fullback and carried three interceptions for 94 yards. The graduation of quarterback Ralph Guglielmi allowed Hornung to emerge as a star in 1955. He amassed 1,215 total yards and led Notre Dame to an 8–2 record.

What followed was perhaps the most unusual Heisman Trophy-winning season on record. Although he could not keep the injury- and graduation-depleted Fighting Irish from stumbling to eight losses in ten games, Hornung was a one-man dynamo in 1956.

The senior passed and ran for 354 yards against Southern Cal—the best single-game total in the nation. He finished among NCAA leaders with 1,337 total yards.

He tallied more than half of his team's points and, on defense, made two interceptions to raise his career total to ten. When told he had out-pointed Tennessee's Johnny Majors for the Heisman, Hornung was—perhaps for the only time in his life—almost speechless. "I didn't think I was even up for consideration," he admitted.

Hornung graduated to a Hall of Fame career with the Green Bay Packers. A hard-living, hard-playing style that might have worn out others worked just fine for the Golden Boy. He played several positions, won three NFL scoring titles, and was named NFL Player of the Year in 1960 and 1961.

One of the best all-around players ever to suit up for the Irish, Paul Hornung remains the only Heisman Trophy winner to play for a losing team. Notre Dame was 2–8 in 1956.

Fall from Grace:
The Kuharich and Devore Years

Joe Kuharich's passion for Notre Dame football could not be questioned. As a boy growing up in South Bend, he often raced to Cartier Field after school to soak up the atmosphere. He came to know Knute Rockne. He pretended he was the Fighting Irish star du jour in local sandlot games, sometimes using bound-up rags as a football.

Though small, Kuharich was an aggressive player who starred at Riley High School and bulked up to play guard for the Fighting Irish in the 1930s. He fulfilled his dream when he was hired to coach his hometown team and alma mater in 1959. That dream quickly turned into something of a nightmare.

In his defense, Kuharich did not inherit great talent from outgoing coach Terry Brennan. Notre Dame was coming off a 6–4 season and was two years removed from a 2–8 campaign. Other programs were catching up to the Irish, who were no longer a cinch to nab the top Catholic players in the country and whose high academic standards made recruiting a challenge. Kuharich did not thrive under the circumstances.

His 1959 team secured back-to-back wins over Iowa and Southern Cal in the closing weeks to salvage a 5–5 record. But his 1960 squad did the unthinkable, losing eight consecutive games after an opening win over California. It remains the longest stretch of futility in Fighting Irish history, and it prompted *Time* magazine to run a feature on the team that November asking, "What's wrong with Notre Dame?"

"Caught between a tough schedule and tough academic standards," the article surmised, "Kuharich may be able to produce an occasional good season, but the golden days of Notre Dame are likely to be gone forever."

Though the magazine correctly pointed out the hurdles an aggressive schedule and strict admission requirements posed for Notre Dame's football program, it turned out to be incorrect on two counts. Kuharich never did manage to produce "an occasional good season," at least not by Notre Dame's expectations. His teams went 5–5 in 1961 and 1962. And despite the fact that he was given a vote of confidence with a contract extension after his second season, the school was relieved when Kuharich resigned in the spring of 1963 to become supervisor of NFL officials.

And, of course, the golden days were hardly "gone forever." After assistant Hugh Devore filled in (for the second time in his career) to coach the 1963 squad to a 2–7 record, a new "Ara" dawned.

A Scholastic review of the 1959 season recounted a 5–5 record under first-year coach Joe Kuharich with George Izo calling the shots at quarterback.

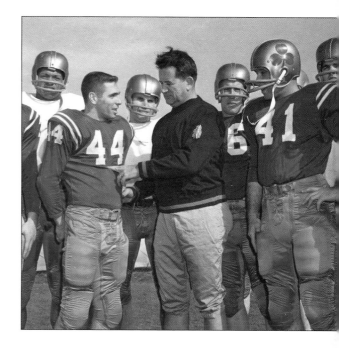

Joe Kuharich addresses his Fighting Irish squad in 1961. A 5–5 record that year matched his high-water mark at the school, where his pro-coaching techniques did not translate to Notre Dame's usual level of success.

Everybody's All-Americans

Five "Golden Domers" won Heisman trophies in the 1940s and 1950s. But several of their teammates were every bit as vital to producing the most dominant era in Fighting Irish history. Here's a look at six of those All-Americans:

Bob Dove, End (1940–42): Notre Dame's first sophomore starter in seven years, Dove was a two-time consensus All-American. He was named the nation's top lineman in 1942 and was inducted into the College Football Hall of Fame in 2000.

Bill "Moose" Fischer, Guard (1945–48): "Moose" followed George Connor as Notre Dame's second Outland

Bob Dove, a two-time All-American and the 1942 Rockne Trophy winner as the country's best lineman, poses with Notre Dame mascot Clashmore Mike.

George Connor was a consensus All-American in both seasons that he played for the Irish and never lost a game.

Trophy winner. He was voted the nation's top interior lineman in 1948. He captained that squad and was also named captain in the East–West Shrine Game. He was inducted into the College Football Hall of Fame in 1983.

George Connor, Tackle (1946–47): Connor played for the College of the Holy Cross in 1942 and 1943 but transferred to Notre Dame after the war. A rock-solid 6'3" and 230 pounds, he paved the way to back-to-back national titles, won the first Outland Trophy in 1946, served as captain in 1947, and was called by Frank Leahy the greatest defensive lineman he ever coached. He was inducted into the College Football Hall of Fame in 1963.

(Center): *All-American sweaters were in high style at Notre Dame in the 1940s and '50s.*

Quarterback Ralph Guglielmi was a unanimous All-American and finished fourth in the Heisman Trophy balloting in 1954.

Emil Sitko, Halfback (1946–49): He became known as "Six-Yard" Sitko for his per-carry rushing average. A 23-year-old freshman in 1946, Sitko led the Irish in rushing for four straight years—once while playing fullback. During that span, Notre Dame posted a 36–0–2 record and won three national titles.

Bob Williams, Quarterback (1948–50): At 19, Williams was the youngest man on Notre Dame's varsity when he coaxed the Irish to ten straight wins and a national title in 1949. Against Michigan State, he completed 13 of 16 passes (including two scoring strikes), booted a 50-yard punt that went out of bounds on the four-yard line, and ran 40 yards for a touchdown.

Ralph Guglielmi, Quarterback (1951–54): Frank Leahy ranked "Goog" among the greatest passers in Notre Dame history. He won a starting job three games into his freshman year. He also threw for more than 3,000 yards and intercepted ten passes in his career. He was inducted into the College Football Hall of Fame in 2001.

Monograms Come in All Colors

African Americans had made an impact on college football long before many schools, particularly those in the South, began to integrate in the 1950s and 1960s. Harvard and Amherst had black players in the late 1880s, and George Jewett was Michigan's fullback in 1890. Notre Dame suited up a handful of black players in the first half of the 20th century, but none played enough to earn a varsity letter until 1953.

That year, a priest caught lineman Wayne Edmonds off-campus and asked him what he was doing there. "I went to get a haircut," Edmonds replied, noting that his skin color prevented him from getting one at the on-campus barbershop.

The football team was more accommodating. Coach Frank Leahy promised Edmonds's family in Pennsylvania that he would look out for Wayne, and he had help from his players. Teammates entered restaurants and stadiums at Edmonds's side. If one would not be allowed on an opponent's field, Leahy said, then none of his players would suit up. Notre Dame went 9–0–1 with Edmonds backing up Art Hunter at tackle.

"All these other teams we beat, people said they were supposed to be leaders," Edmonds told student newspaper *The Observer*. "But Notre Dame was a real leader."

Lineman Wayne Edmonds became the first African American to earn a monogram at Notre Dame.

Derby-style hats and Fighting Irish pennants were in vogue at Notre Dame Stadium during the 1950s.

Die-hard Irish fans supported their team by sporting a variety of ribbons and buttons, some decked out with good luck charms.

Until the leprechaun was officially adopted as Notre Dame's mascot in 1965, Irish terriers had the run of campus. This stuffed one went by the name "Terry."

Although the look of Notre Dame pennants has changed over the years, the hearts of the fans who wave them and pin them to their walls have not.

RUDY, THE JOES, AND THE ERA OF ARA

1964–1985

Notre Dame success came in powerful pairs in the 1960s and '70s: two extraordinary Joes—Theismann and Montana—and two national title-winning coaches—Ara Parseghian and Dan Devine. These were among the greats who led Notre Dame to three national championships (1966, 1973, 1977) and six bowl game victories during the 1970s.

Ara Parseghian is carried off the field after a Sugar Bowl win that secured Notre Dame the 1973 national championship.

This button signaled fans' exuberance over a new direction for Fighting Irish football.

*Vagas Ferguson (32) lowers his shoulders in a 1978 game against Miami.
Ferguson led Notre Dame in rushing with back-to-back 1,000-yard seasons.*

Ara Wastes No Time

Ara Parseghian was the first great Notre Dame football coach who did not attend the school, which seems rather odd, considering how the Miami of Ohio product has come to embody the winning tradition of the Fighting Irish.

Downplaying talk that he was the man who rescued Notre Dame from mediocrity and returned it to the top of college football, Parseghian has said he feels mixed emotions when people reminisce about the "Era of Ara," a period that included Fighting Irish national championships in 1966 and 1973.

"It does allow a light humorous pride to reflect against a slight embarrassment," he wrote in the foreword to *Notre Dame's Era of Ara*, a book penned by his longtime friend Tom Pagna. "In honesty, it is being human enough to enjoy the high praise meant, and more human in realizing that it is not totally deserved."

Born in 1923, Ara Raoul Parseghian was the youngest of two sons born to French and Armenian parents. He was named after an ancient king who came to represent Armenia's struggle for freedom. His parents had

no way of knowing that the *A* in his first name would one day be so aptly replaced by an *E* when Notre Dame football fans fondly recall an 11-year stretch that featured 95 victories, 17 losses, and 4 ties.

How destined was Parseghian for the Notre Dame coaching job? In 1941, a classmate wrote in his high school yearbook, "He will become football coach at Notre Dame."

Ara honed his leadership skills in the U.S. Navy during World War II, earned All-American honors as a halfback at Miami of Ohio, and played briefly for the Cleveland Browns. He assisted Woody Hayes at his alma mater in 1950 then took over the program when Hayes left to become Ohio State's head coach the following year.

Parseghian led Miami to a 39–6–1 record over five seasons. And although in eight subsequent years at Northwestern his record was barely above .500 (36–35–1), four of his wins came in consecutive years against Notre Dame. The Irish took notice and turned that yearbook sentiment into a prophecy when they hired him as their head coach in 1964.

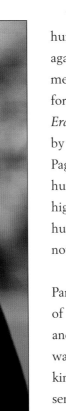

Ara Parseghian was named after an Armenian king, and he received a royal reception when he took over as Irish head coach in 1964.

Under Ara Parseghian's watch, there would be no stripes or shamrocks on Notre Dame's gold helmets.

> **"In our early staff meetings at Notre Dame he told us, 'If we're organized I think we can win five games, because we are much deeper than at Northwestern. If we do a super job we could win seven. And with a little luck we might even go 10–0.' He came close to being exactly right."**
>
> **—Tom Pagna, longtime Parseghian aide**

Parseghian won two national championships, including one in 1966 when his Irish played Duffy Daugherty's (left) Michigan State Spartans to a memorable draw during the regular season.

Desperate for a change, Notre Dame students were elated. They chanted, "Ara! Ara! Ara!" in the middle of South Quad. They gave their new coach a ten-minute standing ovation at halftime of a basketball game. That was before Parseghian had even put his superb motivational and organizational skills to the test in a single game.

Nevertheless, Ara did not disappoint. His impact on the field was as immediate as his popularity. By shuffling players around to new positions, drilling his men into the best shape of their lives, installing a pro-style offense, and removing the stripes and shamrocks from the jerseys and helmets in favor of a more traditional look, Ara reinvented a team that went 2–7 in 1963 and started his career in South Bend with nine straight wins. That 1964 Irish team was 1 minute, 33 seconds from a perfect 10–0 season and a national title when a Southern Cal touchdown toss gave the Trojans a 20–17 win in Los Angeles, spoiling the dream debut. "I prefer to think of it as a 9¾ to ¼ record," Parseghian quipped.

More Important Victories

Ara Parseghian's greatest challenges have come far away from the football field. And while he and his family have lost dearly, they continue fighting.

Between 1997 and 2005, Parseghian lost three grandchildren—Michael, Christa, and Marcia—to Niemann-Pick Type C, a neurodegenerative disease with no known cure. They were the children of Ara's son Mike and daughter-in-law Cindy.

Parseghian has driven wins on and off the field with his charitable work.

Ara, who has been raising money for multiple sclerosis research and treatment since learning in 1967 that his daughter Karan had the disease, established the Ara Parseghian Medical Research Foundation in 1994. As of March 2007, more than $27 million had been raised, and scientists funded by the organization have identified a gene known to cause Niemann-Pick Type C.

"During my years of coaching football," Parseghian said in a plea for help on his Web site (www.parseghian.org), "each spring was dedicated to recruiting and rebuilding my team, and each fall was dedicated to fighting for every yard to be victorious. At this time in my life, that process has particular significance, but we are no longer playing a game."

Along the way, Parseghian discovered untapped talent in Heisman Trophy-winning quarterback John Huarte and receiver Jack Snow, who went on to set several school aerial records. Others followed them to the forefront. "Coach gave us each a chance to show what we could do," Snow said.

National championships were built on 9–0–1 and 11–0 records in 1966 and 1973, respectively. And the '69 and '70 squads lost just one regular-season game each.

No, Ara did not attend Notre Dame. He was not even Catholic. But to Fighting Irish fans, he was something even better. He was the man who put Notre Dame football back on top.

1964 Heisman Trophy Winner John Huarte

John Huarte was, perhaps, the least likely Heisman Trophy winner in the history of the award. He did not play enough in his junior season to earn a monogram. He was so soft-spoken, teammates had a hard time hearing the plays he called in the huddle. And in the spring of 1964, after he had been named starting quarterback by first-year coach Ara Parseghian, Huarte separated his throwing shoulder in a scrimmage. Three team doctors called for surgery, which could have sidelined him for his senior slate.

Parseghian suggested he visit a specialist in Chicago, a former football player who recommended letting time serve as healer. A beaming Huarte heeded that doctor's advice, rested the arm over the summer, arrived in South Bend ready to play in the fall, and led Notre Dame to one of its most surprising seasons.

"Ara used to joke that the whole 'Rudy' story could've been made about me," Huarte said in 2005, "because that was Ara's first season, we'd gone 2–7 the year before, and I barely had any experience. So no one expected much of me or the team."

Parseghian saw something special in Huarte. Granted, he did not have many quarterbacks from which to choose. Still, the way the quiet 6'0", 180-pounder surveyed

John Huarte did not play enough to earn a letter in 1963 but became Notre Dame's sixth Heisman Trophy winner the following season.

defenses and threw the ball had the coach convinced his offense might have some zip.

It did. With his confidence soaring, Huarte threw for 270 yards and two long touchdown passes to teammate Jack Snow in an opening 31–7 upset of Wisconsin. It was the first of nine straight victories, eight of which were decided by more than two touchdowns.

All that stood between Notre Dame and a national championship was rival Southern Cal, Huarte's hometown team. The quarterback coolly led his squad to a 17–0 halftime lead, but the Trojans left Huarte and the Irish heartbroken, scoring 20 points in the second half, including the winning touchdown with 1:33 remaining.

Huarte received a more pleasant shock days later when a phone call informed him that he was the sixth Heisman Trophy winner in Notre Dame's history. His 12 school records helped him edge Tulsa's Jerry Rhome as the top player in the country.

Huarte played sporadically as a pro, joining the ranks of Boston, Philadelphia, Minnesota, Kansas City, and Chicago in a career that spanned the late '60s and early '70s. He was as surprised in 2006 upon his enshrinement in the College Football Hall of Fame as he was more than 40 years earlier when he won the Heisman Trophy.

The Leprechaun

One need not be Irish to don the green cutaway suit and country hat of Notre Dame's leprechaun mascot. All that matters, according to cheerleading coach Jo Minton, is that one's blood runs blue and gold.

Minton said that's why, in 1999, she never thought twice about choosing Michael Brown, Notre Dame's first black leprechaun. What matters, she noted, is that the "candidate has the right heart to be the person who represents Notre Dame."

The Fighting Irish have fielded at least two leprechauns of Hispanic descent, including Mexico City native Juan Muldoon in 2006. There are actually two leprechauns chosen each spring after a grueling tryout process that includes physical fitness tests, a mock media session, simulated game cheering, and a 15-minute individual interview. The top finisher earns the honor of brandishing the shillelagh at football and men's basketball games, while the runner-up counts soccer, volleyball, hockey, and women's basketball among his cheering duties.

"I've always had a penchant for going nuts during football games," top 2006 leprechaun Kevin Braun told school newspaper *The Observer*.

If "going nuts" at games plays to the advantage of Notre Dame's leprechauns, the same could not be said for previous mascots. Irish terriers served in that capacity in the early years, when taming the mascots was more important than turning them loose to fire up the crowd. In 1963, one of the dogs even appeared on the cover of a university publication with Coach Hugh Devore and captain Bob Lehmann.

Late cartoonist Ted Drake, from nearby Elkhart, Indiana, took the Notre Dame mascot in an animated direction in 1964 when the leprechaun he drew for the football team's pocket schedule made the cover of *Time* magazine that same year. With that kind of national publicity, it was no wonder Notre Dame adopted the leprechaun as its official mascot in 1965.

For more than 40 years, the leprechaun—usually shown from the side with fists raised—has served as one of the most recognizable symbols in college athletics. He is said to bring Notre Dame's teams good luck and magical powers, a claim that some Fighting Irish foes might not dispute.

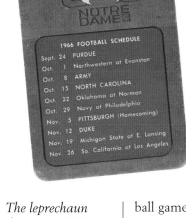

The leprechaun drawn in 1964 by Indiana native Ted Drake has remained largely unchanged. The pipe, however, was eventually removed.

Since the 1960s, Notre Dame's leprechaun has led the cheers—and the team onto the field—at Fighting Irish football games.

Leprechaun hats are in style year-round in South Bend, not just on St. Patrick's Day.

The looks, outfits, and names have changed through the years, but calling for Purdue as a main ingredient in Irish stew has been rather constant, as it was during this game in 1979.

A winged leprechaun was associated with Notre Dame as early as the 1940s. Here, one sits atop Navy's Tecumseh statue on a 1949 game program.

BABE RUTH STADIUM   BALTIMORE   OCTOBER 29, 1949

NAVY–NOTRE DAME

50¢

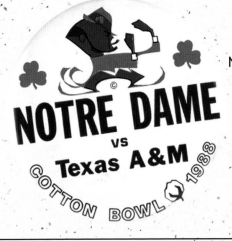

NOTRE DAME
vs
Texas A&M
COTTON BOWL 1988

Notre Dame's leprechaun has come in many variations, but the fists-up pose is a familiar one.

FISK TIRES AND THE ABC RADIO NETWORK PRESENT

NOTRE DAME FOOTBALL 1965

date	team
September 18	California
September 25	Purdue
October 2	Northwestern
October 9	Army
October 23	USC
October 30	Navy
November 6	Pittsburgh
November 13	North Carolina
	Michigan State
November 20	Miami

PROPERTY OF THE NOTRE DAME FIGHTING IRISH

Irish lighter aside, Notre Dame opted for a nonsmoking leprechaun after the original was drawn with a pipe.

Mike Brown, Notre Dame's first black leprechaun, tips his bowler to the crowd at a 2000 home game.

Mascots merged in 1965 when the leprechaun—Robert Guenard of Boston—joined forces with Clashmore Mike III on the sidelines.

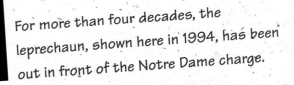

For more than four decades, the leprechaun, shown here in 1994, has been out in front of the Notre Dame charge.

1966: Notre Dame 10, Michigan State 10

ABC Sports was flooded with 50,000 letters and a petition signed by 20,000 fans begging the network to air the 1966 Notre Dame–Michigan State game nationally. The Irish had used their allotment of national TV dates, so the game was scheduled to air only regionally. Given the outcry, ABC persuaded the NCAA to allow a tape-delayed broadcast in the blacked-out areas. "It was. . . as big as any Olympics, there was so much publicity," recalled Andy Sidaris, who directed the telecast.

Fans flooded both campuses all week, soaking up the festive atmosphere before the November 19 meeting in East Lansing between the No. 1-ranked Irish and No. 2-ranked Spar-

In what some called the "Game of the Century," Irish linebacker John Pergine gets in the face of Michigan State quarterback Jimmy Raye (16).

tans. But the pregame buzz soon stood in stark contrast to stunned silence in the stands following a 10–10 tie, perhaps the most talked-about draw in college football history.

Michigan State took a 10–0 lead on a Regis Cavender touchdown run and a 47-yard Dick Kenney field goal in the second quarter. Notre Dame's lone touchdown came on a 34-yard Coley O'Brien pass to Bob Gladieux before halftime. Joe Azzaro pulled the Irish even on a 28-yard field goal to open the final period.

Notre Dame, without All-American halfback Nick Eddy, lost quarterback Terry Hanratty, center George Goeddeke, and Gladieux in one of the hardest-hitting games ever played. Those injuries, and the virtually impenetrable Michigan State defense of Bubba Smith, George Webster,

Jess Phillips, and Charlie Thornhill, entered Ara Parseghian's mind when the Irish coach called his final plays.

With the ball at their own 30-yard line and 1:24 on the clock, the Irish made four straight runs, absorbed a sack, and ran out the clock on a quarterback sneak. "We fought hard to come back and tie it up," Parseghian explained of his decision to play it safe. "After all that, I didn't want to risk giving it to them cheap."

The Outcry: Old Notre Dame Will Tie Over All

Headlines screamed "Tie, Tie for Old Notre Dame" and "Old Notre Dame Will Tie Over All," among other witticisms following the 10–10 stalemate between Michigan State and Notre Dame in 1966.

"No one really expected a verdict in that last desperate moment," wrote Dan Jenkins in *Sports Illustrated.* "But they wanted someone to try."

Such coverage prompted a magazine-burning demonstration on Notre Dame's campus. And while Michigan State's players and fans and Irish critics everywhere jumped on Ara Parseghian for playing it safe in the final two minutes, the Notre Dame coach has stood by his decision for more than 40 years.

On November 19, 1966, No. 1 Notre Dame and No. 2 Michigan State battled to a famous draw, but it was the Irish who came out on top in the year-end polls.

Parseghian called it one of the greatest comebacks in Notre Dame history. "The last thing Duffy Daugherty or I wanted was a tie," he added.

But while Michigan State's season was over at 9–0–1 because of a rule prohibiting them from making back-to-back Rose Bowl trips, the Irish had one more game to play—and one more chance to impress the poll voters. They crushed Southern Cal 51–0 in the season finale, earning the national championship.

1966 National Championship Season

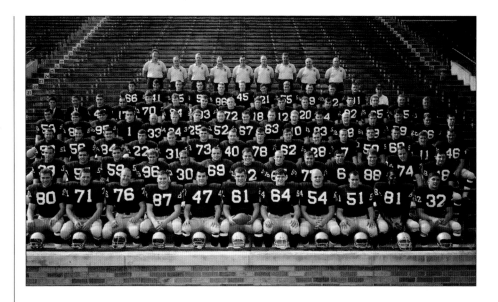

The Beatles played San Francisco in their last concert before a paid audience, *Star Trek* debuted on NBC, and Jerry Lewis hosted his first annual Muscular Dystrophy Association Telethon as school was convening in 1966. On the Notre Dame campus, the bigger news was a battle between sophomores Terry Hanratty and Coley O'Brien. The winner would call signals for a promising team that featured stars such as Nick Eddy, Jim Lynch, Tom Regner, Alan Page, and Rocky Bleier.

Unaware at the time that both young quarterbacks would figure hugely in his first national title, Coach Ara Parseghian opted for Hanratty, who was two inches taller than O'Brien.

Notre Dame's November trip to Michigan State, a game that would spark as much pregame and postgame chatter as any in history, was not on anyone's mind as the 1966 season dawned. Of far greater concern was an opener against Bob Griese and Purdue, a game that set the tone for Parseghian's third Irish season.

It was a day that belonged to Hanratty and sophomore classmate Jim Seymour, who was 6′4″, 200-plus pounds, and ran like a gazelle. "I would just love to see them try to cover Seymour one-on-one," Parseghian said.

Little that Purdue tried worked. Hanratty, outperforming Griese, completed 16 of 24 passes for 304 yards. Seymour snared 13 balls for 276 yards, setting a school receiving record. The Irish prevailed 24–16.

If the Hanratty-to-Seymour connection was devastating, Notre Dame's defense was even more dominant. Lynch and Page pounded the opposition as the Irish shut out six of their remaining nine foes. For the year, only Purdue and

Michigan State managed more than a touchdown against the Irish, who compiled a 362–38 scoring advantage.

Notre Dame overcame its share of adversity, too. The day before the No. 1 vs. No. 2 game at Michigan State, leading rusher Eddy slipped stepping off the train and was sidelined with a shoulder injury. Hanratty and center George Goeddeke were knocked out of the game in the first quarter, leaving O'Brien to save the day.

A legendary 10–10 stalemate with the Spartans left the Irish to answer questions about their coach's decision to play for a tie in the closing minutes. They saved their best response for the field, concluding a 9–0–1 season with a 51–0 romp at Southern Cal.

"I vowed to bring back a national championship for the student body someday," said Parseghian after his team was voted No. 1 in the AP and UPI polls. "I didn't know how soon or when, but I vowed I would do it."

A dozen members of Notre Dame's 1966 national championship team earned All-American honors of some variety.

Joe Theismann: Rhymes with Heisman

As Notre Dame's longtime sports information director, Roger Valdiserri was always on the lookout for new ways to market the Fighting Irish. In 1967, one arrived in the form of a 148-pound, not-quite-six-foot-tall quarterback named Joe Theismann.

The name was pronounced "Theeseman," but after Joe's sophomore season, Valdiserri suggested an upgrade. "Thighsman," he said, smelling a future promotional campaign, "as in Heisman." After some ancestral digging, Joe found out that "Thighsman" was the original pronunciation after all, but it had been changed when the family arrived in America. His grandmother set the record straight.

Some people might have cringed. Not Theismann. He just smiled. Notre Dame Assistant Coach Tom Pagna said of Theismann, "[A] guy hasn't been born with more confidence in himself than Joe Theismann. He felt he could do anything he set his mind to. And . . . he was almost right."

What Theismann lacked in size he made up for in every other area. He had big hands and a strong, accurate right arm. He saw plays before they developed. He was quick on his feet. His wiry frame made him durable; defenders could never seem to measure him for a big hit. Given his size and skills, he would have made an outstanding pro baseball player. In fact, in 1971, he was drafted by the Minnesota Twins but turned down a career in baseball for his first love, football.

Theismann took over for injured All-American Terry Hanratty with three games to play in 1968, his sophomore season, and immediately took charge of the huddle. He led the Irish to blowout wins over Pittsburgh and Georgia Tech and a 21–21, season-ending tie with Southern Cal as Notre Dame finished 7–2–1.

The "Theismann for Heisman" campaign reached high gear in 1969 and 1970. He led Notre Dame to 8–1–1 and 9–1 regular-season records and back-to-back Cotton Bowl games. He finished second in the nation in total offense as a senior, setting 12 school records. His 526-yard passing day against USC in his final regular-season game established an Irish record.

Despite all of these accomplishments, Theismann finished second to Stanford quarterback Jim Plunkett in the 1970 Heisman Trophy balloting. He never won the coveted trophy but instead went on to a record-setting career with the Washington Redskins that included an NFL Most Valuable Player Award and a Super Bowl championship in 1983.

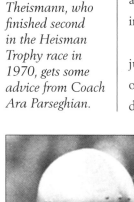

All-American quarterback Joe Theismann, who finished second in the Heisman Trophy race in 1970, gets some advice from Coach Ara Parseghian.

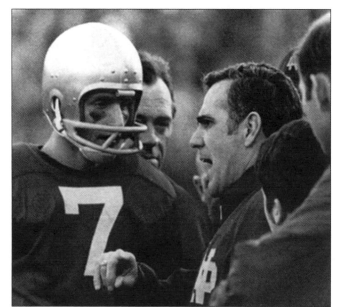

A fan shows off his "Theismann for Heisman" button. Despite setting 12 school records and passing for 526 yards against USC as a senior, Theismann settled for second place in the Heisman voting behind Stanford QB Jim Plunkett.

(Right): *Theismann took over for the injured Terry Hanratty in 1968. Here, he rolls out in a 21–21 tie at Southern Cal that season.*

The Irish Go Back to Bowling

Notre Dame broke a self-imposed 45-year ban on bowl games when it agreed to face Texas in the Cotton Bowl on January 1, 1970. Administrators said revenues would help fund minority scholarships. In the short term, Joe Theismann was the main benefactor.

Notre Dame's junior quarterback broke Roger Staubach's Cotton Bowl passing record with 231 yards in a 21–17 loss to the Longhorns. His 279 total yards also set a new standard for the event.

Theismann and the Fighting Irish enjoyed the New Year's Day 1971 rematch even better. In his last college game, Theismann ran for two touchdowns and threw for another as Notre Dame ended top-ranked Texas's 30-game winning streak with a 24–11 upset victory.

The Irish stopped the Longhorns from claiming a second straight national title by forcing nine fumbles and recovering five. They held the vaunted Texas wishbone attack to 216 rushing yards—more than 150 below its season average—and its lowest point total in three years.

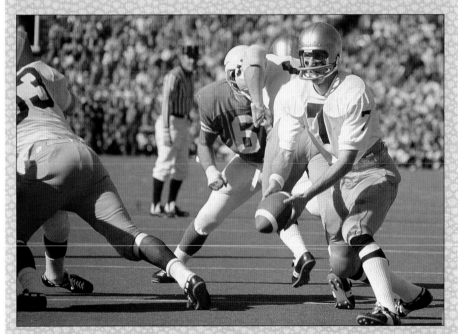

Two terrific Cotton Bowl performances against Texas, including an upset win over the Longhorns in 1971, furthered Theismann's legacy at Notre Dame.

All-Americans of the Era

Quarterbacks John Huarte, Terry Hanratty, Joe Theismann, and Joe Montana passed Notre Dame to national prominence in the 1960s and '70s. They could not have done so without All-American support from virtually every angle. In 1966, Hanratty was one of 12 Irish players who garnered some form of All-American recognition. Following is a glance at some of Notre Dame's top honorees from 1964 to 1985.

Nick Eddy, Halfback (1964–66): Eddy led the Irish in rushing in 1965 and 1966, which helped the latter squad win a national title. He was also the team's top kickoff returner in '66 and finished third in the Heisman Trophy voting that year.

Jim Lynch, Linebacker (1964–66): This sure tackler (255 career stops) won the 1966 Maxwell Award after captaining the Irish to the national championship. He was elected to the College Football Hall of Fame in 1992.

In 1977, Ken MacAfee was a Walter Camp All-American as well as an Academic All-American.

Tom Regner, Guard (1964–66): Regner made 68 tackles as a defensive lineman in 1964 before switching to offense. He was even better on that side of the ball, paving the way for the nation's top-scoring offense during the 1966 national title season.

Kevin Hardy, Defensive Lineman (1964–67): Notre Dame's first three-sport monogram winner in 19 years hit .398 for the 1967 baseball team, started in basketball, and became a three-time football All-American.

Tom Schoen, Defensive Back (1965–67): Schoen played quarterback in 1965 before making room for Hanratty. He led the Irish in interceptions and punt

Allen Pinkett (20), shown making a gain against Navy in 1983, was the first Notre Dame player to break the 4,000-yard rushing threshold.

returns in 1966 and 1967 and set multiple Fighting Irish records for punt returns and punt return yardage.

Tom Gatewood, Split End (1969–71): This speedy split end set virtually every school receiving record while leading the team for three straight years. He still holds the single-season mark for receptions per game (7.7 in 1970).

Ross Browner, Defensive End (1973–77): A dominant force on two national title teams, Browner won the 1976 Outland Trophy for the nation's best interior lineman, the 1977 Lombardi Award as the best lineman in the country, and the 1977 Maxwell Award. The two-time All-American set school records for tackles by a front-four lineman (340) and fumble recoveries (12) and was a 1999 College Football Hall of Fame inductee.

Ken MacAfee, Tight End (1974–77): This College Football Hall of Famer caught 54 passes for 797 yards and six scores in 1977, finishing third in the Heisman Trophy chase.

Bob Golic, Linebacker (1975–78): As a two-time wrestling All-American, Golic compiled a 54–4–1 record. He pinned ball carriers just as surely. His 146 tackles and three interceptions led the 1977 Irish to the national title. He was a captain and a unanimous All-American in 1978.

Vagas Ferguson, Halfback (1976–79): The first Irish player to rush for 1,000 yards in back-to-back seasons,

Ferguson set a school record in 1979 with 1,437 rushing yards. He finished his college career with a record 3,472 rushing yards, including 255 against Georgia Tech in 1978.

Allen Pinkett, Tailback (1982–85): Pinkett was the first to break the 4,000-yard career rushing barrier at Notre Dame. He set several other school records, including carries in a game (40) and in a career (889) and 100-yard rushing games in a season (9).

In addition to winning the Maxwell Award for the best college football player in the country, Jim Lynch was also an Academic All-American in 1966 and a two-time All-American for the Irish.

Nick Eddy led Notre Dame in rushing in 1965 and 1966 and finished third in the Heisman voting in the latter year, after running the Irish to a national championship.

Ross Browner (89) won the Outland, Lombardi, and Maxwell awards during his stellar career as one of the most feared defensive forces in college football.

Game Day

Notre Dame was a different place in the 1960s and 1970s. What college campus wasn't? Vietnam War protests, the Civil Rights movement, and a general questioning of authority became the norm on college campuses. Sideburns and psychedelic music came in and out of vogue. Gender rights became a talking point, too, especially after the first women were admitted to Notre Dame in 1972.

"Coeds were becoming commonplace, and they were giving the school a different personality," wrote Tom Pagna, an Irish assistant coach under Ara Parseghian from 1964 to 1974. "And for some reason, football fit in perfectly with this new look.

"The students were once again enchanted by the fall football pageantry. For longtime Fighting Irish fans it was like the 'good old days.'"

Football may have seemed less important to some for a while, but once Parseghian turned things around, the scene on football weekends began to look much like it does today. Packed pep rallies, band renditions of the "Victory March," tailgate parties, and long lines at the bookstore were the norm.

In addition, the $9 million, 16-story Memorial Library—one of the largest college library buildings in the world—was built near the football stadium in 1963. From inside the stadium, fans and players could look out at the library's mural of Christ towering over the end zone with his arms raised over his head. They gave it a special moniker: "Touchdown Jesus."

The "Word of Life" mural that adorns Notre Dame's Hesburgh Library is better known to football fans as "Touchdown Jesus."

Among life's certainties: death, taxes, and sellout crowds of 59,000-plus at Notre Dame Stadium during this era.

Sometimes, students got a little too wrapped up in the success of the football team. As university president, Father Theodore Hesburgh delivered a warning in 1965 that he would consider ending intercollegiate competition if displays of poor sportsmanship continued. The caution came in response to an apparent attack by students to the Michigan State band's bus the previous year.

Hesburgh got his point across. Eliminating the football program was never a realistic option, of course. Administrators and faculty members were as wrapped up in the team as the students. And that's saying nothing of the alumni pilgrimages, which seemed to skyrocket once the program got back on a winning path in the mid-1960s.

"It's as if they can't get enough of the team," James Armstrong, Notre Dame alumni secretary, told *The New York Times* in 1964. "Many of the alumni will come in Thursday night and won't leave until Monday."

By Tuesday, many were no doubt planning their next football weekend.

1973 National Championship Season

Tom Clements (2) passed himself into Irish football lore with his from-the-end-zone completion to Robin Weber that sealed Notre Dame's 24–23 win over Alabama in the 1973 Sugar Bowl.

Family matters to Tom Clements. He grew up in a family of doctors and lawyers near Pittsburgh, hoping to match the success of his parents and siblings. And so it was on New Year's Eve 1973, after leading the Irish to victory in the Sugar Bowl and securing a national title, Clements recalled the season-opening shutout of Northwestern, after which he learned that his teenage sister Alice had been struck and killed by a car.

"Football had to be the least important thing in the world at this time," said Assistant Coach Tom Pagna, "but he didn't show it. . . . Tom's family was a close group. They were deep and loved in a way that makes family something special."

It was a special year at Notre Dame. Clements made sure of it. Coming off a disappointing 8–3 season in 1972, Coach Ara Parseghian promised better. His team was ranked near the bottom of the Top Ten during the first half of the season. But a 14–10 win over Michigan State and a 23–14 triumph over Southern Cal that ended the Trojans's 23-game unbeaten streak were colossal tests.

Clements was a proven leader, but the rushing of Wayne Bullock and tight-end play of Dave Casper were examples of an offense coming together at the right time. The Mike Townsend-led defense held eight foes to ten points or less.

Finishing the schedule with lopsided wins over Navy, Pittsburgh, Air Force, and Miami vaulted Notre Dame to third in the polls. The Irish trailed top-ranked Alabama and a 10–0–1 Oklahoma team that was on NCAA probation and thus ineligible for postseason bowls. With a Sugar Bowl win over the Crimson Tide, the Irish could claim their first title since 1966.

Clements hit Pete Demmerle on three big pass plays on a first-quarter touchdown drive, and Al Hunter returned a kickoff 93 yards in the second quarter as the Irish took a 14–10 lead. Alabama pulled ahead twice in the second half, but both times Notre Dame answered—on an Eric Penick touchdown run and a late 19-yard Bob Thomas field goal that gave the Irish a 24–23 edge.

On third-and-eight from the Irish two-yard line with less than two minutes to play, Parseghian gambled. Clements backed into the end zone and fired a 35-yard bomb to Robin Weber, a tight end who had caught only one pass all season. "A win or punt situation," Parseghian called it. The Irish won. And the Clements family celebrated.

Ara Parseghian and Notre Dame edged Bear Bryant and Alabama in a 1973 Sugar Bowl contest between two battle-tested programs vying for the national title.

1975 Orange Bowl: The End of an Ara

The highs were high in 1974. Notre Dame's football team was celebrating a national championship. Less than three weeks into the year, the basketball team livened up the party by shocking UCLA, ending the Bruins's record-breaking winning streak at 88 games.

The lows were low in 1974. Over the summer, six Notre Dame football players—all African Americans— were kicked off the team for having a woman in a men's dormitory after hours. Some called it rape, though unfairly as no charges were filed. Others called it racism, suggesting that white players might have been punished less severely.

Ara Parseghian had not been feeling well. His football team had enjoyed the highs of an early No. 1 ranking and the lows of losses to Purdue and Southern Cal. The latter, in the regular-season finale, had deflated everyone in blue and gold. The Trojans outscored the Irish 49–0 in the first 17 minutes of the second half, rallying from a 24–6 deficit to a 55–24 rout in a turnaround that defied logic.

Though Parseghian had decided at midseason that he would resign, the announcement was not made until December 15. "I find myself physically exhausted and emotionally drained," Parseghian said.

But there was one more hurdle to tackle, and it was a familiar one.

Top-ranked Alabama had won 43 of its last 47 games, which included a 24–23 loss to the Irish in the Sugar Bowl during the previous season. The Crimson Tide was a nine-point favorite entering the rematch in the Orange Bowl on January 1, 1975. Many expected a blowout.

Instead, the Fighting Irish sent Ara out a winner by a 13–11 score.

Senior defensive back Reggie Barnett, who had made no secret of his opposition to Notre Dame's suspension of his teammates, said the Irish set any differences aside in the days leading up to the game. "We were talking about how it was Coach's last game," said Barnett, whose late interception kept Alabama from attempting a game-winning field goal. "And how it would be nice to win it. A lot of guys wanted to get it together."

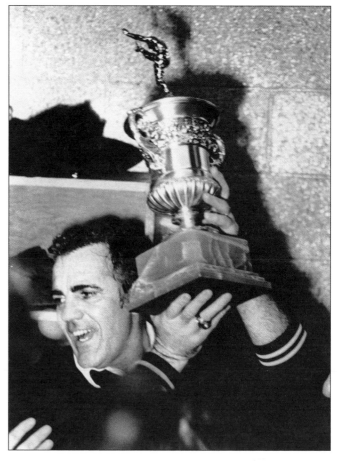

The "Era of Ara" came to an end with the ninth-ranked Irish upsetting No. 2 Alabama 13–11, allowing Parseghian to hoist Orange Bowl hardware after his last game.

Notre Dame took a 13–3 lead, then held on through a frantic fourth quarter. Alabama's powerful rushing attack managed only three first downs via the run.

"I told them they didn't owe me anything," Parseghian said of his players. "They owed it to themselves, and they won it that way."

"Ara Was Fine, But Dan's Devine"

For some, it was a day for ribbons and celebration in South Bend when Dan Devine brought his NFL experience to the Irish in 1975.

Dan Devine accomplished something that no other man in Notre Dame football history has managed: He won a national title in the footsteps of a coaching legend. Others tried and failed. Hunk Anderson won 63 percent of his games after Knute Rockne's death, and Terry Brennan posted a 64 percent success rate following Frank Leahy. More recently, Bob Davie won 58 percent in the shadow of Lou Holtz.

But Devine had better incoming credentials than most. He'd led the Green Bay Packers to a 10–4 record and division title in 1972. And though his four-year record with the NFL club was sub-.500, Notre Dame fans were pleased to be landing a coach with experience at the highest level. In fact, some fans couldn't wait to welcome the new coach. A banner in the stands at the 1975 Orange Bowl (Parseghian's last game with the Irish) said it loud and clear: "Ara Was Fine, But Dan's Devine."

"We're going to be a very young, inexperienced team," Devine said of his first squad in 1975, "but eventually we'll put it all together."

Devine had won previously at Arizona State and Missouri, where the pressure was nothing like it was in South Bend. He learned the difference right away, when back-to-back 8–3 (regular) seasons met with little celebration.

The father of seven would never be as revered as Rockne or Leahy, nor as popular as Parseghian, but Devine was a survivor. His 1977 team overcame an early-season loss to Ole Miss to win a national championship. His 1978 team started with back-to-back losses but finished with a 35–34, last-play Cotton Bowl victory over Houston that ranks among the greatest comebacks in history. And in 1980, his final Irish squad went ten straight games without suffering a loss. His record with the Fighting Irish was 53–16–1.

Those critical of Devine, a detail-oriented man who insisted on pressed pants and shined shoes, were usually comparing him to his predecessor. A 1980 *Washington Post* column explained: "Parseghian was emotional and easy to identify with. Devine is low-key and distant. Parseghian was colorful and glib. Devine is colorless and often fumbles for words."

Still, Devine found success at every stop. He brought the first black players to Arizona State and Missouri before taking the Green Bay job. His college teams went 7–3 in bowl games, and 94 percent of his four-year players graduated.

"He knew who he was, what he wanted to do, and how to get it done," longtime Penn State coach Joe Paterno said.

Devine died in 2002, at age 77.

> **"He did not have Ara's charisma, but his record was as good. I respected him as a man and a coach."**
>
> **—Reverend Edmund Joyce, former Notre Dame executive vice president and the man who hired Dan Devine**

Devine directs quarterback Joe Montana on the sideline during Notre Dame's 49–19 defeat of USC in 1977. The Fighting Irish went on to win the national championship that year.

An autographed Ara Parseghian card is a valuable asset to any collector of Notre Dame memorabilia.

ARA PARSEGHIAN

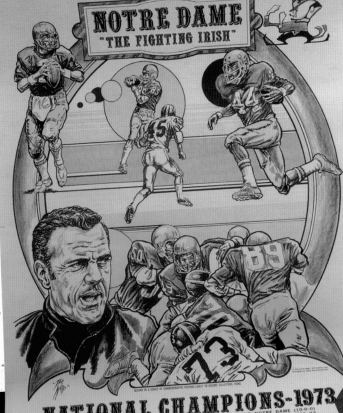

NOTRE DAME "THE FIGHTING IRISH"

NATIONAL CHAMPIONS-1973

IN THE SUGAR BOWL DEC. 31, 1973 BETWEEN ALABAMA (11-0-0) AND NOTRE DAME (10-0-0) WITH THE LEAD CHANGING HANDS SIX TIMES, THE FINAL SCORE WAS: N. D. 24 — BAMA 23

Only 1,000 autographed "Joe Montana, A Golden Tradition" commemorative cards were produced by Upper Deck.

This poster celebrates Notre Dame's 1973 national championship as well as its 24–23 win over Alabama in the Sugar Bowl.

Irish coach Ara Parseghian poses with USC's famous mascot, Traveler, on Notre Dame's campus.

UNIVERSITY OF NOTRE DAME
1973
SELECTED BY THE
FOOTBALL WRITERS ASSOCIATION OF AMERICA

The Football Writers Association of America awarded Notre Dame its 1973 national championship trophy.

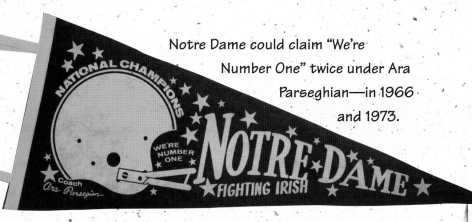

National Champions — WE'RE NUMBER ONE — Coach Ara Parseghian — NOTRE DAME FIGHTING IRISH

Notre Dame could claim "We're Number One" twice under Ara Parseghian—in 1966 and 1973.

HOME EDITION

VOL. CII, NO. 282

The South Bend Tribune

SOUTH BEND, INDIANA, MONDAY, DECEMBER 16, 1974

Departments — Features

PRICE TEN CENTS

Ara Resigns as N.D. Coach
DAN DEVINE NEXT

By JOE DOYLE
Tribune Sports Editor

Dan Devine, long-time successful coach at Missouri and Arizona State and for the last four years coach of the professional Green Bay Packers, was to be named Notre Dame football coach later today.

Devine will replace Ara Parseghian, who announced his resignation Sunday after 11 years as head Irish coach. Parseghian will conclude his 11 years when Notre Dame, ranked No. 8 nationally, plays Alabama (No. 1 in the UPI poll) in the Orange Bowl on New Year's Night.

Ara Parseghian

Dan Devine

Break Deadlock on Oil
U.S., France in Accord

Auto Layoffs

DETROIT (UPI)—American Motors Corp. said today it plans to stop all car production for a week in January because

Parseghian's exit and Devine's arrival were big headlines everywhere and front-page news in The South Bend Tribune.

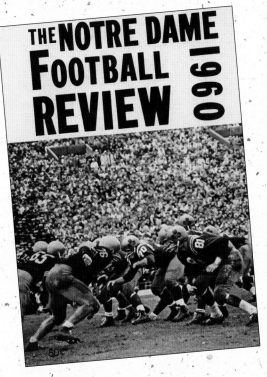

THE NOTRE DAME FOOTBALL REVIEW 1960

50¢

Notre Dame's 1960 campaign ended with a dismal 2–8 record, but a season-ending, 17–0 upset of USC was a bright spot.

NOTRE DAME · WEST STAND
GATE 11 E · SEC. 57 · ROW · SEAT 20

NOTRE DAME VS IOWA
IOWA STADIUM
SAT., NOV. 23, 1963 · 1:30 P.M.
ADMIT ONE $5.00—NO REFUND

NOV. 23

The November 23, 1963, game between Notre Dame and Iowa was never played. It was canceled due to the assassination of President John F. Kennedy.

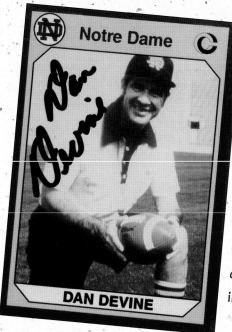

Notre Dame

DAN DEVINE

Dan Devine put his autograph on this football card and his stamp on Irish history by winning a national championship in 1977.

RUDY! RUDY! RUDY!

Daniel "Rudy" Ruettiger turned a few seconds of playing time into a lifetime of glory. He did so with a never-say-die attitude that turned a 5'6", Chicago-area power plant worker into a walk-on football player at Notre Dame who had his name chanted and was carried off the field after finally getting into a game. Hollywood took care of the rest.

"I'd tell people about Rudy," said his former roommate Pete Murphy, "and they thought I was making up a story."

Rudy, the 1993 motion picture that warmed the hearts of Domers and even tugged at the heartstrings of those who root against the Fighting Irish, did have a heaping share of make-believe. Coach Dan Devine agreed to be painted as a villain for Hollywood's sake, when in fact, it was his idea to send Ruettiger in for the final moments of his last home game. And no Irish player ever set his jersey on Devine's desk as a way of sacrificing his place on the "dress list." Rudy was dressing for the game all along.

"Anybody who knows me knows that if any kid came in and put his jersey on my desk," Devine said, "he'd never see it again."

This much is true: Ruettiger had no business getting in to Notre Dame based on his academic record, but he hit the books at nearby Holy Cross Junior College and, after three rejection letters, was admitted in 1974. He told a skeptical Ara Parseghian he would make the team, and he did, by sacrificing his undersized body on every play. Rudy served on the scout team in Parseghian's final season and Devine's initial one, finally attaining his dream of running through the Notre Dame tunnel in uniform on November 8, 1975, in a 24–3 victory against Georgia Tech.

Players and fans did chant "Rudy! Rudy! Rudy!" in the closing seconds, and Ruettiger's improbable quarterback sack is depicted quite accurately by actor Sean Astin in the movie—the first motion picture since 1940's *Knute Rockne All American* to gain Notre Dame's permission for on-campus filming. After the game, Ruettiger was indeed carried off the field—and on to a life that now includes regular motivational speeches and a permanent place in college football lore.

Ruettiger's message: "You don't choose character. It comes alive under adversity."

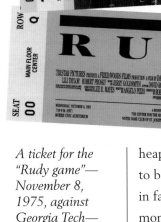

A ticket for the "Rudy game"— November 8, 1975, against Georgia Tech— went for $9. That's not much more than a ticket to see Rudy the movie in 1993.

From Rudy's yearbook photo, one might not have guessed that Ruettiger was a 5'6" member of the Irish scout team.

Pins signifying Rudy's football exploits and his graduation from Notre Dame were worn by movie patrons upon the film's 1993 release.

After recording a quarterback sack against Georgia Tech on the final play of the last home game of his senior year, Ruettiger was carried off the field by his teammates.

1977 National Championship Season

An early loss to Ole Miss did not keep the Fighting Irish from claiming the national championship with a 10–1 record and a Cotton Bowl victory in 1977.

Sports Illustrated had predicted a title for the 1977 Fighting Irish, and a 19–9 opening win against defending national champ Pittsburgh was just what the magazine had in mind. But a 20–13 home loss to unranked Mississippi in the second game of the season had followers of the blue and gold searching for answers.

"When we arrived as freshmen, we told each other we would all have a national championship ring before we left Notre Dame," said Steve Orsini, who, along with fellow captains Willie Fry, Ross Browner, and Terry Eurick, called a players-only meeting after the loss to Ole Miss. "It was gut check time. We...knew that we were a lot better than we had been playing."

Several things went right for Notre Dame in the ten-game winning streak that followed. Third-year coach Dan Devine turned the offense over to quarterback Joe Montana—who sported jersey No. 3—in the third quarter of game three. Montana rallied the Irish from a ten-point deficit to a 31–24 victory against Purdue and later engineered another dramatic fourth-quarter comeback at Clemson.

That heralded defense put up a wall, holding six regular-season opponents to ten points or less. An inexperienced offense found its groove, beginning with a 49–19 thrashing of Southern Cal in which—as a motivational

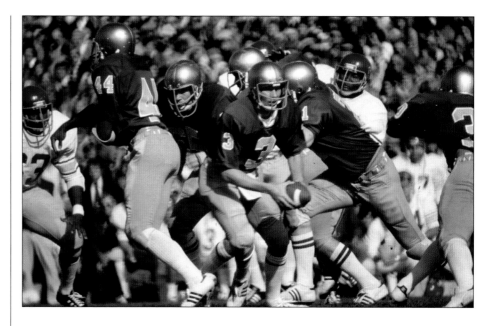

ploy—Devine sent the Irish onto the field in green jerseys for the first time in 15 years.

Facing top-ranked Texas and a potential steamrolling by running back Earl Campbell in the Cotton Bowl, Notre Dame turned five consecutive Longhorn turnovers into scores in a 38–10 win. The blackboard in the Irish locker room said it all following that Cotton Bowl victory:

"It's not where you start," someone had scrawled, surely reflecting a theme that was discussed in the team's September meeting. "It's where you finish.... And you finished on top."

The following day, it was official. Notre Dame had edged Alabama to finish on top for the first time since 1973, earning the national championship nod from the Associated Press writers and the United Press International coaches' panel.

Joe Montana (3) was the "Comeback Kid" during Notre Dame's 1977 national title season, although there was no need for an Irish comeback in this one-sided 49–19 victory over USC.

Joe Montana: The Comeback Kid

Even with his blond hair, boyish good looks, catchy name, and his pedigree from western Pennsylvania—that hotbed of quarterback greatness—none of it would have earned Joe Montana a place among Notre Dame's legendary quarterbacks were it not for the magical fourth-quarter performances delivered time and again by No. 3.

"How many people are there in the world, three billion?" said Jeff Petrucci, Montana's high school quarterback coach, in describing the electricity Joe brought to the huddle. "And how many guys are there who can do what he can do? Him, maybe [Dan] Marino on a good day. Perhaps God had a hand in this thing."

Montana, who saw no varsity action as a freshman, became Notre Dame's "Cardiac QB" as a sophomore in 1975. He came off the bench late in the final quarter at North Carolina and turned a 14–6 deficit into a 21–14 victory in just 62 seconds of playing time. The next week, he entered the game with the Irish trailing Air Force 30–10 in the fourth quarter. Montana ran for one score, passed for another, and set up a Jerome Heavens touchdown for a 31–30 triumph.

He might not have been the biggest, fastest, or strongest-armed quarterback,

Joe Montana did not possess the strongest arm in college football, but his mobility, accuracy, poise, and knack for winning made him a natural leader.

Montana had good looks, charisma, and a golden touch when it came to winning football games. Not surprisingly, he was a fan favorite.

but Montana's ability to lead a team downfield in key situations was unmatched.

"When the pressure came," former teammate Dave Waymer told *Sports Illustrated*, "we knew he was the guy who wouldn't overheat."

Montana missed the 1976 season with a shoulder injury and began 1977 as a third-stringer until desperation set in. Trailing by ten points against Purdue, Montana was called off the bench, engineered a 31–24 win, and passed Notre Dame all the way to a national title.

In 1978, his senior year, Montana directed two come-from-behind regular-season wins and a 35–34 Cotton Bowl thriller over Houston, in which the Irish rallied for 23 points in the fourth quarter—a comeback that defied logic.

That is, all logic but this: Joe Montana was the quarterback. As long as that was the case, the Irish were always within striking distance.

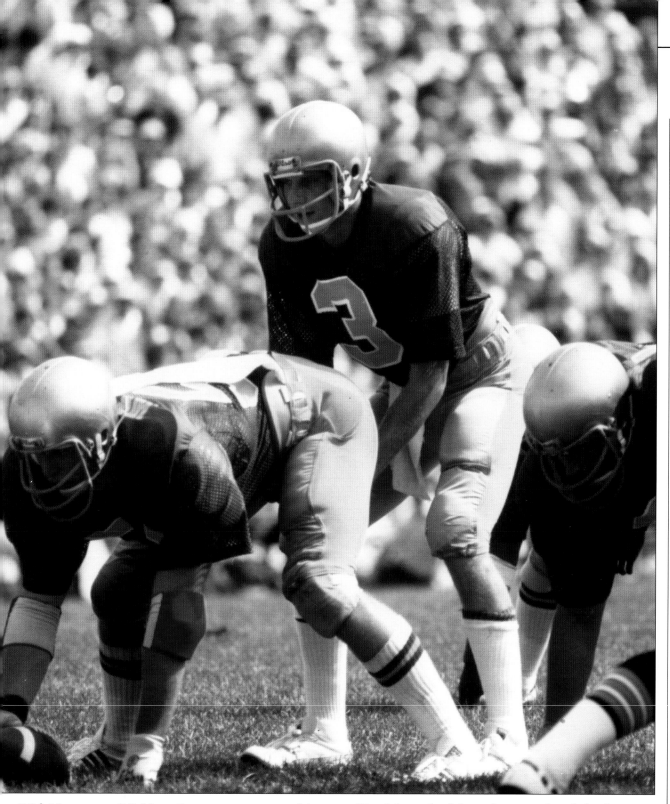

With Montana at QB, Notre Dame was never out of the game. His ability to lead the Irish to come-from-behind victories was unsurpassed in school history.

Montana's Magic Act Got Even Better

His legendary Notre Dame comebacks and national championship ring notwithstanding, Joe Montana was not considered a surefire NFL prospect. In 1979, San Francisco drafted him in the third round as the 82nd pick overall. The 49ers got a steal.

The "Montana Magic" was not limited to South Bend. In 1981, his first full year as starting quarterback for San Francisco, Montana led the team to a

If Montana's signature on this helmet seems unique, so were the quarterback's skills when games were on the line.

13–3 record, found Dwight Clark for "the catch" that sent the 49ers to the Super Bowl, and finished the job with a 26–21 win over Cincinnati for the title. It was the first of four Super Bowl championships Montana directed. He was named MVP in three of those games and led a 92-yard, last-minute touchdown drive to beat the Bengals in the other.

The two-time NFL MVP engineered 31 fourth-quarter comebacks over 15 seasons, gaining acclaim as perhaps the greatest clutch quarterback in football history. Montana was enshrined in the Pro Football Hall of Fame in 2000.

1979 Cotton Bowl

For all of Joe Montana's chills and thrills, it was the right foot of Joe Unis that forever secured a place for the 1979 Cotton Bowl as one of the greatest comebacks in the history of college football.

Sure, it was Montana who rallied Notre Dame from a 34–12 deficit in the waning 7 minutes 25 seconds against Houston on an icy New Year's Day in Dallas, where wind chills made it feel like –6°F at kickoff. It was Montana who, on the final play of his last collegiate game, zipped a ball to Kris Haines on an eight-yard sideline route for the tying touchdown as the clock read 0:00.

Out trotted Unis—a 5'8" junior from Dallas—to kick the most important extra point of his life. He did, but an illegal procedure penalty against the Irish forced him to do it again. Unfazed by the pressure, the swirling winds, or the extra five yards because of the penalty, Unis split the uprights again for a 35–34 Notre Dame victory.

Irish coach Dan Devine called it "the greatest of all the comebacks I've been associated with." Others have called it the "Chicken Soup Game," because Montana was fed the old-fashioned remedy to help combat flu symptoms that had kept him out for most of the third

One of the most amazing comebacks in college football history saw Joe Montana rally Notre Dame for 23 points in the final 7:25 for a 35–34 Cotton Bowl win against Houston in 1979.

quarter and had him swaddled in blankets in the locker room.

Down by 22 points in the fourth quarter, some might have wondered why the shivering quarterback returned to the field at all. Even Montana, the king of comebacks, wouldn't be entertaining thoughts of victory under those circumstances. Or would he?

A blocked punt that Steve Cichy returned 33 yards for a touchdown midway through the fourth quarter gave the lethargic Irish the lift they needed. Montana then led a 61-yard drive, running the final three yards for a touchdown. Two-point conversions after each score made it 34–28.

When Houston recovered Montana's fumble with 1:50 on the clock, Irish hopes appeared dashed. However, Cougars coach Bill Yeoman decided to go for it on fourth-and-one from his own 29-yard line, and Notre Dame's Joe Gramke stopped Emmett King for no gain. "We were kicking the ball only 10 or 12 yards into the wind," Yeoman explained.

Suddenly, Montana was in his comfort zone, with 28 seconds to cover 29 yards. His penultimate pass to Haines fell incomplete with two seconds left, but Montana would not accept failure.

"Joe asked me if I could beat [the defender] again and I said, 'yes,'" Haines later recalled. "He smiled and said, 'Let's do it.'"

Unis did the rest.

Ticket-holders with Irish allegiances did not have much reason to cheer for three-and-a-half quarters on a frigid day in Dallas. Then lightning struck.

The Gerry Faust Years

New York Yankees owner George Steinbrenner served as toastmaster at Notre Dame's 1985 football banquet. That night, even in the presence of one of the most contentious and colorful figures in sports, defensive tackle Eric Dorsey said of outgoing coach Gerry Faust, "He's gone through more controversy than anybody I've ever been associated with."

There was controversy from the start with Faust. Notre Dame, accustomed to having their pick of big-name college and even professional coaches, turned to the high school ranks to hire him as Dan Devine's replacement in 1980. His record at Cincinnati Moeller was untouchable—174–17–2, with seven undefeated seasons. Still, the leap from high school football to any major college program is a great one. And add the pressure of coaching at Notre Dame? It was a gamble that failed.

Allen Pinkett (20) was the focal point of the offense during the Gerry Faust years. He became the first Irish player to rush for 4,000 career yards.

In five years, Faust (30–26–1) lost more games than any coach in Irish history (at the time), surpassing Joe Kuharich by three setbacks. His best stretch saw Notre Dame go 6–4–1, 7–5, and 7–5 from 1982 to 1984, making trips to the Liberty Bowl (1983) and Aloha Bowl (1984). Through all the misery, Faust remained the friendliest man and most optimistic coach one might ever meet. He was living his dream, and he could frequently be found on a kneeler at the Grotto, silently expressing thanks for it.

The highlight of Faust's career came on November 6, 1982, when his unranked Irish visited Pittsburgh and dismantled Dan Marino and the top-ranked Panthers, 31–16. Freshman running back Allen Pinkett rushed ten times for 112 yards on his way to several career records under Faust.

The lows reached their lowest in 1985, when "Oust Faust" T-shirts circulated on campus, listing the schedule as a "Farewell Tour." Faust resigned before his last game—a trip to Miami that saw the Hurricanes hammer away at an already wounded man. They kept their regulars on the field until late in a 58–7 thrashing. After the debacle, a priest suggested Faust refuse to shake the hand of Hurricanes coach Jimmy Johnson. Without words, Faust extended his hand and shook Johnson's.

One week later, his voice trembled during his final dinner with the team.

"I cherish these five years more than you can imagine," said one of the best-liked yet most vilified coaches in Fighting Irish history. "And I hope that in the years to come I can be in some small way part of the Notre Dame family."

No one cared more about Notre Dame's struggles than Coach Gerry Faust, shown leading the Irish to a 1982 win over Michigan in the first night game at Notre Dame Stadium.

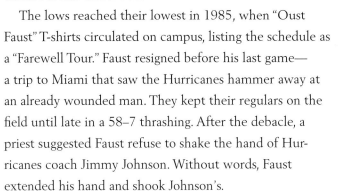

Midwestern Rivals: ND vs. Michigan

No shillelagh or bucket or megaphone is awarded to the winner of the Notre Dame–Michigan game. Each school has a bigger rival: Southern Cal and Ohio State, respectively. Still, in a series that dates back to 1887, it makes perfect sense that the Irish and Wolverines feel something special every time they meet. That something special comes in the form of history, tradition, and a burning desire to crush each other.

Ann Arbor and South Bend are separated by about 175 miles on the map but far less than that in the record books. Michigan stands No. 1 in all-time wins and winning percentage. Notre Dame is No. 2 in each, a mere .007 percent behind in the latter at the start of the 2008 season.

Part of the reason for the slight edge, Irish fans will point out, is the fact that the Wolverines twice stopped

In 1909, the Fighting Irish finally managed to defeat Michigan, the school that taught them how to play football in 1887.

Scoring on Michigan '09.

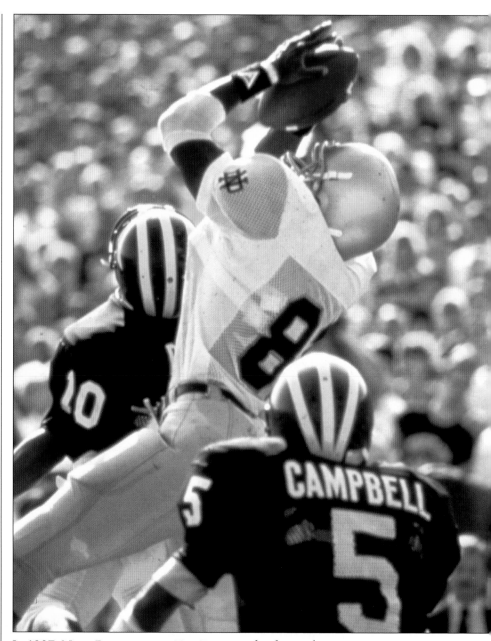

In 1987, Notre Dame receiver Tim Brown took a big performance in a 26–7 win at Michigan and rode it all the way to the Heisman Trophy that season.

After a two-year hiatus, Notre Dame and Michigan resumed their series in 2002, with the Irish defeating the Wolverines 25–23.

scheduling Notre Dame for long stretches. The first came after the Irish snapped a string of eight straight losses to Michigan in 1909. Wolverines coach Fielding Yost hated losing and maintained that the Irish held a competitive advantage due to their independent status. It was a claim that contributed to his falling-out with Notre Dame coach Knute Rockne in the 1920s.

The series resumed in 1942 and 1943, but Michigan coach Fritz Crisler called it quits after that. It was not until 1978, thanks largely to the efforts of Irish athletic director Moose Krause, that Notre Dame and Michigan resumed the series.

"It's good for Michigan, it's good for Notre Dame, and it's good for college football," President Gerald Ford, a former Michigan player, told Krause.

Some of Notre Dame's greatest triumphs over Michigan have come on kicks, none bigger than Harry Oliver's 51-yarder in 1980 to secure a 29–27 Irish victory as time ran out. The previous season, Chuck Male's four field goals made the difference in a 12–10 win in Ann Arbor. And in 1988, it was a late three-pointer from Reggie Ho, his fourth of the game, that gave the Irish a 19–17 edge, starting their drive toward a perfect season.

The Notre Dame–Michigan Series
Michigan Leads 20–14–1

1887—Michigan 8, ND 0	1981—Michigan 25, ND 7
1888—Michigan 26, ND 6	1982—ND 23, Michigan 17
1888—Michigan 10, ND 4	1985—Michigan 20, ND 12
1898—Michigan 23, ND 0	1986—Michigan 24, ND 23
1899—Michigan 12, ND 0	1987—ND 26, Michigan 7
1900—Michigan 7, ND 0	1988—ND 19, Michigan 17
1902—Michigan 23, ND 0	1989—ND 24, Michigan 19
1908—Michigan 12, ND 6	1990—ND 28, Michigan 24
1909—ND 11, Michigan 3	1991—Michigan 24, ND 14
1942—Michigan 32, ND 20	1992—Michigan 17, ND 17
1943—ND 35, Michigan 12	1993—ND 27, Michigan 23
1978—Michigan 28, ND 14	1994—Michigan 26, ND 24
1979—ND 12, Michigan 10	1997—Michigan 21, ND 14
1980—ND 29, Michigan 27	1998—ND 36, Michigan 20
	1999—Michigan 26, ND 22
	2002—ND 25, Michigan 23
	2003—Michigan 38, ND 0
	2004—ND 28, Michigan 20
	2005—ND 17, Michigan 10
	2006—Michigan 47, ND 21
	2007—Michigan 38, ND 0

■ —Played at Notre Dame
■ —Played in Toledo, Ohio
■ —Played at Michigan

Harry Oliver booted a 51-yard field goal as time expired in a 1980 game against Michigan, giving the Irish a 29–27 home victory.

The Biggest Rivalry: ND vs. USC

Between 1983 and 1995, the Irish never lost to the Trojans—an unbeaten streak of 13 games.

No team has beaten Notre Dame as many times as Southern Cal. No team has beaten Southern Cal as many times as Notre Dame. And no series, for either school, has produced as many memorable games as this one.

Notre Dame–USC is the oldest, and greatest, intersectional rivalry in college football. Why? For the reasons mentioned above. For the 14 Heisman Trophy winners who have played in the series—more than in any other. For the fact that the Trojans sought out the Irish in 1926, when other schools were trying to avoid them. For Anthony Davis and Southern Cal's 55 unanswered points in 1974. For Dan Devine's green-jersey scheme in 1977. For the "Bush Push" that broke Irish hearts in 2005.

"When I hear people talk about Ohio State–Michigan or Auburn–Alabama being such huge rivalries, I chuckle," said former Irish All-American Allen Pinkett. "Sure, these are big rivalries, but unless there's something of national significance about one of these games in a particular year… they won't match ND–USC in terms of the attention paid to them across the country."

Little did anyone know in 1926, when Notre Dame edged Southern Cal 13–12, that one of college football's biggest rivalries had just been born.

Here are some of the most memorable games in one of college football's greatest rivalries:

December 4, 1926: ND 13, USC 12—The series' first game was decided in the final minutes. The Irish erased a 12–7 deficit and won the game on a 24-yard TD pass.

November 21, 1931: USC 16, ND 14—Johnny Baker's 33-yard field goal with one minute left gave USC their first win in South Bend and halted Notre Dame's 26-game unbeaten streak. USC started the weekend by visiting the grave of Knute Rockne, who had died earlier that year.

December 6, 1947: ND 38, USC 7—The Irish were ranked first and USC third in this season-ending fight for the national title. Before 104,953 fans in Los Angeles, Notre Dame turned a 10–7 halftime edge into a blowout, finishing the season 9–0 and securing a national title.

October 27, 1973: ND 23, USC 14—En route to Ara Parseghian's second national title, the Fighting Irish had to stop the Trojans's 23-game unbeaten streak. Eric Penick's

In 2005, the heroics of quarterback Brady Quinn (10) resulted in one of the greatest games in the ND–USC series but could not save the Irish from a last-second 34–31 defeat.

85-yard touchdown run early in the third quarter helped Notre Dame avenge a 45–23 loss the previous year.

November 30, 1974: USC 55, ND 24—One of the most dramatic turnarounds in college football history saw the Trojans overcome a 24–0 deficit with 55 straight points. In the first 17 minutes of the second half, USC turned a 24–6 deficit into a romp.

October 22, 1977: ND 49, USC 19—When the Irish returned to their lockers after warming up in South Bend, green jerseys awaited them. Dan Devine's motivational

tactic worked like a charm, as the Trojans had no answers for Joe Montana and the ND attack.

November 26, 1988: ND 27, USC 10—In the first No. 1 vs. No. 2 matchup in series history, Tony Rice and the visiting Irish prevailed, en route to a national title.

October 15, 2005: USC 34, ND 31—Irish QB Brady Quinn ran for the go-ahead touchdown with two minutes to go. But with three seconds left, tailback Reggie Bush shoved his QB Matt Leinart into the end zone from the one-yard line as the top-ranked Trojans won a classic.

The ND–USC Series: Notre Dame Leads 42–32–5

1926—ND 13, USC 12	1946—ND 26, USC 6	1963—ND 17, USC 14	1980—USC 20, ND 3	1997—USC 20, ND 17
1927—ND 7, USC 6	1947—ND 38, USC 7	1964—USC 20, ND 17	1981—USC 14, ND 7	1998—USC 10, ND 0
1928—USC 27, ND 14	1948—ND 14, USC 14	1965—ND 28, USC 7	1982—USC 17, ND 13	1999—ND 25, USC 24
1929—ND 13, USC 12	1949—ND 32, USC 0	1966—ND 51, USC 0	1983—ND 27, USC 6	2000—ND 38, USC 21
1930—ND 27, USC 0	1950—USC 9, ND 7	1967—USC 24, ND 7	1984—ND 19, USC 7	2001—ND 27, USC 16
1931—USC 16, ND 14	1951—ND 19, USC 12	1968—ND 21, USC 21	1985—ND 37, USC 3	2002—USC 44, ND 13
1932—USC 13, ND 0	1952—ND 9, USC 0	1969—USC 14, ND 14	1986—ND 38, USC 37	2003—USC 45, ND 14
1933—USC 19, ND 0	1953—ND 48, USC 14	1970—USC 38, ND 28	1987—ND 26, USC 15	2004—USC 41, ND 10
1934—ND 14, USC 0	1954—ND 23, USC 17	1971—USC 28, ND 14	1988—ND 27, USC 10	2005—USC 34, ND 31
1935—ND 20, USC 13	1955—USC 42, ND 20	1972—USC 45, ND 23	1989—ND 28, USC 24	2006—USC 44, ND 24
1936—ND 13, USC 13	1956—USC 28, ND 20	1973—ND 23, USC 14	1990—ND 10, USC 6	2007—USC 38, ND 0
1937—ND 13, USC 6	1957—ND 40, USC 12	1974—USC 55, ND 24	1991—ND 24, USC 20	
1938—USC 13, ND 0	1958—ND 20, USC 13	1975—USC 24, ND 17	1992—ND 31, USC 23	—Played at Notre Dame
1939—USC 20, ND 12	1959—ND 16, USC 6	1976—USC 17, ND 13	1993—ND 31, USC 13	—Played at Chicago's Soldier Field
1940—ND 10, USC 6	1960—ND 17, USC 0	1977—ND 49, USC 19	1994—ND 17, USC 17	
1941—ND 20, USC 18	1961—ND 30, USC 0	1978—USC 27, ND 25	1995—ND 38, USC 10	—Played in Los Angeles
1942—ND 13, USC 0	1962—USC 25, ND 0	1979—USC 42, ND 23	1996—USC 27, ND 20 (OT)	

Notre Dame faced Syracuse for the first time in 1961, prevailing 17–15 at home, but the Orange returned the favor 14–7 in a 1963 meeting at Yankee Stadium.

The Irish upset Oklahoma 27–21 in their 1952 matchup. Nine years later, Knute Rockne graced the cover of the program before Notre Dame's 19–6 season-opening win.

Bringing back the Four Horsemen for the program cover did not help the Irish in a 1961 home date against Northwestern. The Wildcats won 12–10.

George Gipp would have been proud of the Fighting Irish in their 30–0 kicking of Southern Cal in 1961.

With a slice of Americana on the program for a 1953 "Hall of Fame Game" meeting with Pittsburgh, Notre Dame posted a 23–14 home triumph.

Notre Dame's first bowl game appearance was celebrated on the program cover of a 1963 rematch with Stanford. But this time, it was the Cardinal coming out on top 24–14.

Notre Dame made back-to-back Cotton Bowl trips in 1978 and 1979, and each was memorable. The first, a 38–10 rout of Texas, led to a national title. The second, a 35–34 win over Houston, was among the greatest comebacks in history.

With the leprechaun as a cover boy, Notre Dame had Navy's number in 1954, 1964, and 1968, notching victories against the Midshipmen.

THE MODERN AGE

1986–2007

The path from the waifish, bespectacled Lou Holtz to the imposing, Super Bowl ring-wearing Charlie Weis was a roller-coaster ride for Notre Dame. It featured two of the most dangerous return men in college football history—Tim Brown and Raghib Ismail—and, in Brady Quinn, the most prolific passer ever to wear blue and gold.

Coach Lou Holtz won 100 games at the Notre Dame helm—second only to Knute Rockne— and returned the Fighting Irish to national champion- ship glory in 1988.

In 1987, Notre Dame celebrated its centennial season of football by kicking off the home slate with a win over Michigan State.

Darius Walker and the Irish came storming back in the final minutes for a memorable 20–17 home victory against UCLA in 2006.

The Notre Dame Mystique

There's a good reason goose bumps swell on the skin of Notre Dame fans the instant they step on campus on fall Saturdays. There's a unique spirit alive at the school that even those who are not fans of the Fighting Irish can recognize and appreciate. Some call it the "Notre Dame mystique." But don't ask for a description because an adequate one doesn't really exist.

"I am often asked to explain the mystique of Notre Dame," former Irish coach Lou Holtz said. "I reply, 'If you've been there, no explanation is necessary. If you haven't been there, no explanation will satisfy you.'"

From the hundred or so college offers he received, Joe Theismann had settled on North Carolina State—or at least he thought he had—that is, until Notre Dame asked him to make a second visit to South Bend. He returned home and told his father he was going to play for the Fighting Irish. "He asked, 'Why?'" Theismann recalled. "And I told him, 'I can't give you a specific reason.'. . . It was almost like the university chose me."

When Father Edward Sorin and the Brothers of St. Joseph founded the University of Notre Dame on a plot of snowy northern Indiana land in November 1842, they had no way of knowing that it would be a boorish game—a cousin of soccer and rugby—that would bind Catholics and non-Catholics from all over the world in their love for the school.

Certainly, faith is part of the mystique. As one of the world's leading Catholic universities, Notre Dame is proud of its ties to the Church. The Virgin Mary stands atop the magnificent Golden Dome capping the campus administration building. "Touchdown Jesus," a mural of Christ, dominates the library tower overlooking the football stadium. "We're No. 1" Moses, a statue raising an index finger as if victorious on the gridiron, holds a prominent place nearby.

Each year, thousands visit the Grotto—a replica of France's Lourdes shrine where Mary appeared to St. Bernadette in 1858—to pray and light candles near the two campus lakes, St. Mary's and St. Joseph's. Football

Since 1878, the Grotto—shown here in 1885 (top) and in 1996—has been a sacred place for generations of Notre Dame students, alumni, and visitors to pray and give thanks.

It was an easy walk from one end of Notre Dame's campus to the other in the 1920s.

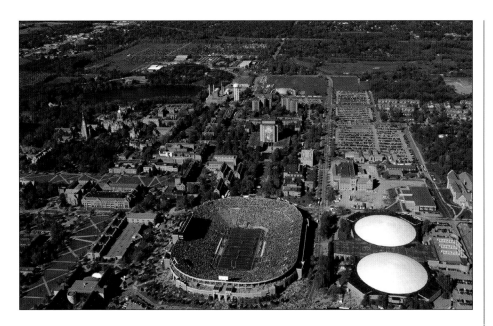

Though the campus has been progressively growing in recent years, Notre Dame remains one of the most scenic college settings in America.

weekend crowds wait patiently for a spot to open at the Grotto's kneelers, many having strolled down the hill after snapping photos and craning their necks to admire the ornate Sacred Heart Basilica.

Of course, the mystique is also very much about football and Notre Dame's history of great teams, outstanding performances, thrilling comebacks, and star players. All over the country, young boys raced home from church on Sundays to hear Lindsey Nelson recount Notre Dame highlights in the 1960s and '70s. Before long, those youngsters were throwing, kicking, and catching footballs in the yard, pretending to be Hornung or Hanratty or Montana. Chances are, their own children were later born into the tradition as well.

"The whole Notre Dame football thing means so much more than just rooting for a college sports team," said Murray Sperber, author of *Shake Down the Thunder: The Creation of Notre Dame Football*. "It's deep and it's profound and often passed down through generations."

Though the Fighting Irish have encountered long dry spells, they have always managed to work their way back to the top, never staying out of the national limelight for very long. And when the Fighting Irish are at or near the top, the rest of the college football world takes direct aim at the blue and gold.

There was a time when the Irish could operate as "gatherers" of talent rather than "recruiters"— a time when virtually every high school football star would jump at the chance to play in South Bend. Now, with more games than ever finding their way to national television audiences and more schools competing for top talent, those days are gone.

Still, the very mention of Notre Dame conjures up the essence of college football itself, and players are still drawn to the spot chosen by Father Sorin in ways that sometimes defy words. As long as student managers gather every week to spray those famed gold helmets with a fresh coat of paint that contains actual gold flakes, as long as the players walk to and from pregame mass through a tunnel of screaming fans hoping to catch a glimpse of their football heroes, and as long as running out of the tunnel at Notre Dame Stadium puts goose bumps on the arms of players and fans alike, the "Notre Dame mystique" remains very much alive.

One of the school's most recognizable landmarks, the Golden Dome was a gift from the sisters of St. Mary's College after the Main Building was destroyed by fire in 1879. The Golden Dome—shown here in 2007 (bottom)—shines as brightly as it did in 1888 (top).

Lou Holtz: Lovable Leader

Despite his self-deprecating public persona, Lou Holtz demanded respect and got it. He returned Notre Dame to glory in the late 1980s after several lackluster seasons.

Lou Holtz is many things: Funny man, master motivator, amateur magician, sought-after speaker. To Notre Dame at the conclusion of the 1985 season, he was something else: The man who could put the school's lackadaisical football feet back on the ground.

Several players slouched in their chairs during Holtz's first meeting with the team he had longed to coach above all others. It was December 1985, two days after the Fighting Irish suffered a 58–7 loss at Miami, and center Chuck Lanza had the misfortune of having his feet propped up against a stage while he inspected his fingernails rather than fixing his eyes on his new coach.

"Young man, how long have you been playing football?" Holtz asked Lanza.

Holtz followed Lanza's answer with a promise. "If you ever want to play another down," he said, "you will put your feet on the floor, sit up straight, and pay attention."

Shoes across the room hit the floor. Chairs shuffled as backs straightened. All eyes focused on the thin, bespectacled man who had led William & Mary, North Carolina

State, Arkansas, and Minnesota to successful turnarounds before landing his dream job at a university whose fight song served as the soundtrack for his early Catholic schooling.

Lanza would become an All-American under Holtz, who in one meeting commanded the respect of his new players, set victory as an expectation, and mapped a course that would lead the Fighting Irish to that destination. And it would start right away, with 6 A.M. workouts that became known as "pukefests" for their level of intensity, which had more than a few players rushing for the restrooms. Those left standing would be equipped, in Holtz's mind, to lead Notre Dame back to college football's summit.

Holtz's mind, as usual, was accurate.

Lou Holtz was born in Follansbee, West Virginia, and grew up in nearby East Liverpool, Ohio. "We needed a raise to be considered poor," he quipped. Far from being the top athlete or brightest student in his class, he developed a quick wit and a willingness to sacrifice his body to survive the taunting of classmates and hits from bigger football rivals, respectively. Holtz did not play much during his college years at Kent State, but his football mind was advanced, and his desire to coach unwavering.

> "Look at me: I'm 5'10", 152 pounds. I wear glasses, speak with a lisp, and have a physique that makes it appear I've been afflicted with scurvy most of my life. I ranked low in my graduating class of 278 coming out of high school. And here I am, a head football coach at Notre Dame."
>
> **—Lou Holtz**

After assisting greats like Woody Hayes at Ohio State and Forest Evashevski at Iowa, Holtz began his head-coaching career at William & Mary and coaxed them to a rare conference crown in 1970. He took North Carolina State to four straight bowl games from 1972 to 1975, led Arkansas to an 11–1 season and No. 3 national ranking in the final 1977 polls, and, in the early 1980s, turned a downtrodden Minnesota program into a bowl qualifier in just two seasons before Notre Dame came calling.

Holtz's quips and magic tricks played well in the media, but his message to his players was rooted squarely in what he considered the fundamentals of football and life: "Block and tackle better than your opponent, and wins will follow. Work tirelessly on the field and in the classroom, and success will be the natural result."

Holtz tips his hat to the crowd after another Irish victory. He guided five of his Notre Dame teams to ten or more wins.

"From the very beginning," said George Kelly, a longtime Notre Dame assistant coach and a special assistant to the athletic director during Holtz's tenure, "he was

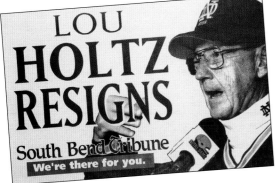

In 1996, Holtz's resignation after a successful 11-year run caused shock waves among Notre Dame fans.

extremely demanding and wanted the squad to know just what sort of hard work would be required to succeed.... Maybe the players didn't realize just how hard they would have to work to make it into that winner's circle." Soon enough, the Irish understood perfectly.

A 1988 national title highlighted an 11-year run in which Holtz won 100 games, lost 30, and tied twice. His successful recruiting, innovative play-calling, and demand for excellence took the Irish to 12–0, 12–1, 10–1–1, and 11–1 seasons. Notre Dame's feet were firmly planted right where fans expected them to be—back at the top.

Lou Holtz Quotebook

Lou Holtz's wit and wisdom made him an expert motivator during his coaching career. He had that Rockne-like ability to turn a team hanging its collective head into a burst-through-a-wall juggernaut with a few choice words. That gift still plays well on the speaking circuit, in his television analyst's role, and in his writing. Here's a sampling of Holtz's philosophies:

🏈 "Discipline is not what you do to someone, but what you do for them."

🏈 "I ask each of you to follow three basic rules: Do what is right. Do your very best. Treat others like you'd like to be treated."

🏈 "If you can trust someone, know he is committed to excellence, and cares about you, hug him, and never let him go, because he is a winner."

🏈 "Ability is what you're capable of doing. Motivation determines what you do. Attitude determines how well you do it."

1987 Heisman Trophy Winner Tim Brown

The odds of Tim Brown winning a Heisman Trophy looked long indeed as he lined up at the Hoosier Dome to receive the first kickoff of Notre Dame's 1984 season. The Dallas native had thought basketball might be his ticket to college before Irish coach Gerry Faust took an interest in his talents as a receiver. When Purdue's kickoff bounced off his chest, slipped between his legs, and was recovered by the Boilermakers, the freshman was ready to trade his cleats for high-tops after one touch of the pigskin.

"I wanted to go home after that," he said years later.

Instead, Brown found a home—as the most accomplished all-purpose yardage man in Notre Dame history and winner of the 1987 Heisman Trophy. He became the first wide receiver in history to win the coveted award.

Truth be told, Brown did as much to get a leg up in the award chase in the last game of the 1986 season—Lou Holtz's first year as Notre Dame's head coach—as he did in his Heisman-winning season. He amassed 254 all-purpose yards and set up the winning score with a 56-yard punt return as the Irish upset No. 17-ranked USC 38–37 in Los Angeles. In one afternoon, Brown stamped himself as the 1987 Heisman favorite.

Early in 1987, the elusive speedster returned back-to-back punts 66 and 71 yards for touchdowns against Michigan State, distancing himself from other contenders. "I've only known one other football player who brings the crowd to its feet every time he touches the ball—Gale Sayers when he was with the Bears," noted former Irish Heisman winner Paul Hornung. "This kid has that same gift."

In 1987, Brown led the Irish to eight wins in their first nine games and averaged 167.9 all-purpose yards per game, despite facing double- and triple-teams on his pass routes and consistently watching opponents kick the ball away from him. It was a far cry from his debut, a long way from the basketball court, and a springboard to an NFL career that could one day land him in the Pro Football Hall of Fame.

Give Tim Brown (81) space in the open field, and he was gone. The elusive receiver and return man was a threat to score every time he touched the ball.

"Catholics vs. Convicts"

It was a game billed by Notre Dame students as "Catholics vs. Convicts"—the upstart Fighting Irish against the brash, top-ranked Hurricanes of Miami, who had routed ND by a combined 133–20 margin in their previous four meetings. It started, fittingly, with a scrap between the teams in the tunnel of Notre Dame Stadium. And then the October 15, 1988, contest became something bigger than the massive hype that preceded it.

In 2005, fans voted it the greatest game in Notre Dame Stadium history.

Miami knew its 36-game winning streak was in jeopardy early in the second quarter when Pat Terrell returned an interception of a Steve Walsh pass 60 yards for a touchdown that gave the Irish a 21–7 lead. However, Walsh rallied with two touchdown passes to tie the game at halftime.

Statistically, Miami held the edge on a mid-70s October day that felt more like southern Florida than northern Indiana. Walsh passed for 424 yards and three scores, and the Hurricanes built a 481–331 edge in total yards. Four lost fumbles and three interceptions, though, proved devastating for the nation's No. 1-ranked team.

Still, Notre Dame waited until the very end to deliver a knockout punch. Miami, trailing 31–24, overcame a controversial fumble near the Irish goal line and scored on Walsh's pass to Andre Brown with 45 seconds remaining in the game. College football did not have an overtime rule at the time, leaving Hurricanes coach Jimmy Johnson with a decision that would affect the national championship picture for the rest of the season.

Johnson never hesitated. Rather than kick an extra point and play for a 31–31 tie, he kept his offense on the field to go for the win with a two-point conversion attempt.

That play remains vivid in the minds of Irish fans everywhere. Walsh dropped back, his linemen providing him plenty of time, and lofted a pass toward running back Leonard Conley. Irish defensive back Terrell read the play, stepped in front of the intended target, and batted the ball harmlessly to the grass.

Notre Dame 31, Miami 30.

"I followed Walsh's eyes the whole way," Terrell, a Florida native and high school rival of Conley's, said after the game. "I knew where he was going to throw the football, and I don't think he saw me coming."

"This was a win by the Notre Dame spirit," added Irish coach Lou Holtz. "A win by the spirit of a group of guys who refused to fold."

The 1988 Miami–Notre Dame game started with an ugly skirmish in the tunnel and turned into one of the most memorable games in school history.

This ticket treated a Notre Dame fan to one of the greatest Irish victories ever—a 31–30 upset of No. 1 Miami that was not secure until Pat Terrell knocked away a two-point conversion pass in the final minute.

1988 National Championship Season

Coach Lou Holtz got a ride off the field after guiding the Irish—who most thought were "a year away"—to a national title-clinching Fiesta Bowl win over West Virginia.

Conventional wisdom said the 1988 Notre Dame football team was a year away from greatness. Most of its best players were underclassmen. Some, like speedster Raghib Ismail, had literally just taken their first steps on campus.

But Lou Holtz is not a big believer in conventional wisdom. The third-year coach asked one thing of his 1988 squad: perfection. The Fighting Irish provided it, winning 12 straight games and their first national championship in 11 years.

"I've underestimated this team in a lot of areas," Holtz said after Notre Dame wrapped up its perfect run with a 34–21 thrashing of previously unbeaten West Virginia in the Fiesta Bowl. "They've done everything I've asked of them. Is this a great football team? I'd have to say yes, because nobody proved it wasn't."

There were close calls, to be sure. It took four clutch field goals from a walk-on, self-described "pre-med geek" named Reggie Ho to upset Michigan 19–17 in the season opener. A trip to Pitt was almost more than the Irish could handle before pulling out a 30–20 triumph. And a thrilling 31–30 shocker over top-ranked Miami hoisted Notre Dame to a No. 2 national ranking, although many "experts" still considered the Hurricanes the most talented team in the land.

The turning point may have come in the hours leading up to Notre Dame's regular-season finale, a showdown against Southern Cal, one of the nation's top teams. Could the Irish win two "games of the year" in back-to-back months? More importantly, could they do it without two of their star players?

Ricky Watters and Tony Brooks, game-changing offensive weapons, were late for the team's Friday dinner. It was not the first offense for either one, so the decision was clear to Holtz, a coach who had suspended three star players from his 1977 Arkansas team after they violated what he called his "do right" rules before the Orange Bowl. He met with his Irish captains, and all agreed that Watters and Brooks would fly back to South Bend instead of suiting up for the game.

Just as Holtz's Razorbacks had rallied to upset Oklahoma 11 years earlier, Notre Dame put forth perhaps its most complete effort of the season to topple the Trojans 27–10. Tony Rice, a quarterback who conquered academic obstacles to gain admission to Notre Dame, hit Ismail with a 55-yard pass on the first Irish play and later ran an option keeper for a 65-yard score. Frank Stams was in on three sacks of USC quarterback Rodney Peete, and Stan Smagala returned an interception 64 yards for a touchdown.

"There was no secret to it," Stams said, noting that Notre Dame's depth of talent and an aggressive game plan formed a devastating combination.

West Virginia would discover the same thing in the Arizona desert during the Fiesta Bowl on January 2, 1989, as Notre Dame's defense held the Mountaineers to their lowest offensive total of the season. Rice outplayed quarterback Major Harris, and offensive spark plugs like Watters, Ismail, running back Mark Green, and tight end Derek Brown proved too much. The Irish never trailed in the game, winning 34–21 to claim the national championship.

"Sometimes it seemed like they had about 16 players on the field," noted West Virginia center Kevin Koken.

The 1988 Fighting Irish aimed for perfection and attained it, winning all 12 games and the national championship.

Leading the Pack

Counting national championships can be a dicey issue. For example, some sources credit Notre Dame with 13 "recognized" national titles, while the Fighting Irish themselves claim only 11. Other schools list more national crowns in their media guides than those same sources acknowledge.

But since 1936, there has been one measurable standard: the Associated Press poll of sportswriters. The following is a list of schools that have won the most AP national championships since the onset of that poll.

Notre Dame 8	Nebraska 4	LSU 2
Oklahoma 7	Ohio State 4	Michigan 2
Alabama 6	Texas 3	Penn State 2
Miami 5	Army 2	Pittsburgh 2
USC 5	Florida 2	Tennessee 2
Minnesota 4	Florida State 2	

The Irish team that was "a year away" reached its perfect destination right on time, historically speaking. Knute Rockne, Frank Leahy, Ara Parseghian, and Dan Devine had each won a national title in his third season at the Notre Dame helm. That Holtz joined the list came as little surprise to those who followed his career.

"If somebody had an assignment to mold a Knute Rockne and a Frank Leahy, they couldn't have done a better job than Lou Holtz," said Dick Rosenthal, Notre Dame's athletic director at the time. "He *is* Notre Dame."

And Notre Dame, perfection in hand, was back on top in college football.

A convincing Fiesta Bowl win gave Notre Dame its eighth AP national title. No school has captured more.

1988 NOTRE DAME 1988

National Champions

12-0

ND -19 MICHIGAN -17	ND -30 PITTSBURGH -20	ND -22 NAVY -7
ND -20 MICH. STATE - 3	ND -31 MIAMI -30	ND -54 RICE -11
ND -52 PURDUE -7	ND -41 AIR FORCE -13	ND -21 PENN ST. - 3
ND -42 STANFORD -14	ND -34 WVU -21	ND -27 SO. CALIF. -10

Coach Lou Holtz

There were some close calls along the way, but the Fighting Irish knocked off a dozen foes on their way to the 1988 national title.

In addition to winning the AP national championship, the 1988 Fighting Irish earned this trophy for finishing No. 1 in the coaches' poll.

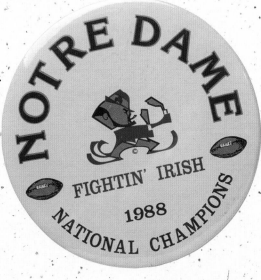

NOTRE DAME
FIGHTIN' IRISH
1988
NATIONAL CHAMPIONS

An 11-year wait came to an end when the 1988 Fighting Irish returned to the top.

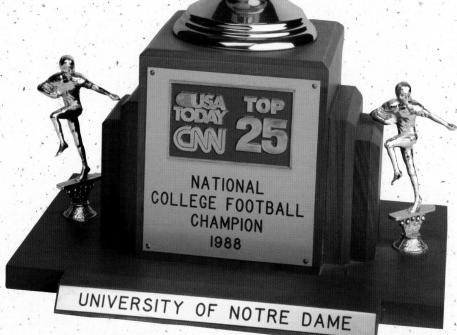

USA TODAY CNN TOP 25

NATIONAL COLLEGE FOOTBALL CHAMPION 1988

UNIVERSITY OF NOTRE DAME

THE ARIZONA REPUBLIC
TUESDAY, JANUARY 3, 1989   C

FIESTA BOWL

Fighting's done: Irish are No. 1

Notre Dame linebacker Arnold Ale hits West Virginia running back Craig Taylor on an incomplete pass during the second quarter of Monday's game at Sun Devil Stadium.

W. Va. dreams crushed

By Bob Eger
The Arizona Republic

Those probably weren't echoes reverberating across Sun Devil Stadium on Monday. Only cheers.

And it wasn't thunder that shook down from above. Just a few raindrops.

But if Notre Dame's Fighting Irish didn't wake up the echoes and shake down the thunder, they did about everything else.

The top-ranked Irish destroyed third-ranked West Virginia, 34-21, in Sunkist Fiesta Bowl XVIII and claimed their eighth national college football championship and first in 11 years.

A crowd of 74,911, the largest in stadium history, plus a national television audience on NBC saw the Irish put the finishing touches on an unbelievable season.

The team that was supposed to be a year away from greatness finished 12-0 for the first time in the school's long and storied history.

In the process, the Irish beat Miami (Fla.) when it was ranked No. 1, Southern California when it was ranked No. 2 and West Virginia when it was ranked No. 3.

This probably wasn't a matter of West Virginia (11-1) not being ready for prime time.

It was more that the Mountaineers were not ready for Notre Dame.

The Irish had a 16-0 lead comfort-

January 2, 1989, was a long day in the desert for the previously undefeated West Virginia Mountaineers.

The most recent Notre Dame national title was pennant-worthy indeed.

FIESTA BOWL EXTRA   1989

Phoenix Gazette

MONDAY, JANUARY 2, 1989   50¢

IRISH WIN!

8th national championship

1943   1946   1947   1949   1966   1973   1977   1988

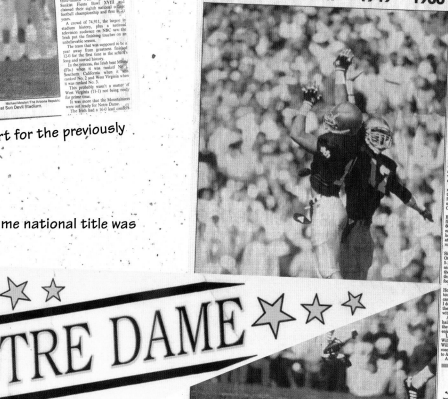

Notre Dame Fighting Irish player Ricky Watters gives a high-five salute to a teammate after an earlier victory this season.

Notre Dame photo via Phoenix Gazette

Irish eyes smiling on Holtz

Lou Holtz
Notre Dame coach

From Phoenix Gazette news services

The stories never run dry on Lou Holtz, the comic/magician/ticket-seller who among coaches football now at Notre Dame.

Most of the yarns are unrelated to what this leprechaun of a human has done in propelling the Irish out of frustration and back into the No. 1 ranking in college football and their eighth national championship.

The tales expound on his abilities to arouse a football team, to elevate players to their peaks on a given day, to alleviate tension in the biggest moment of a 21-year-old's life.

A common story is told about Holtz's list of 107 things he wants to do in life, written in 1966 after he was fired as an assistant at South Carolina, when his wife was pregnant with their third child.

Holtz has achieved all but 22. He has now won a national championship, seen the Pope, had dinner at the White House, appeared on the Johnny Carson show, made a hole-in-one and seen the Coliseum in Rome.

Not on his list was the Bookstore Basketball Tournament, the largest five-on-five tournament in the world, a 686-team, single-elimination event held each spring at Notre Dame. When Holtz heard so many students watched from atop the bookstore one year that the roof caved in, he formed a team.

It's the most important thing here, Holtz said, speaking of the basketball tournament, not No. 1. It's never canceled — rain, snow, sleet or tornado. I do all right until we get to the final 32, then I'm out of my element. I'm all right with those engineering students.

And the slender man with the blond hair combed down on his forehead and the wire-rim spectacles leans back and enjoys a long guffaw.

Lou Holtz has moved players from William and Mary in 1969 ("I coached William, and a couple other guys coached Mary") to North Carolina State to Arkansas and Minnesota.

At those places he played Humpty

Lou Holtz
Notre Dame coach

Birth date: Jan. 6, 1937.

Hometown: Follansbee, W.Va.

College: Kent State University and the University of Iowa.

Record: 129-75-5

Family: Wife, Beth; children, Luanne Altenbaumer, Skip, Kevin and Elizabeth.

Career highlights: Began his head-coaching career in 1969 at William and Mary at age 32. He also was head coach at North Carolina State, Arkansas and Minnesota. He was head coach of the New York Jets in the National Football League in 1976. Fourteen of the 19 collegiate teams under his direction have earned post-season bowl invitations and nine have finished in the final AP Top 20.

Dumpty, putting the pieces together again. He's become a master at infusing new life into gasping, dying football programs.

Long before he was known for his one-liners, he lifted William and Mary into its only bowl game. He escalated North Carolina State into the Top 10, a place it has not occupied since. He revived a Minnesota program that had lost 17 straight Big Ten Conference games.

Now Holtz has resuscitated the Fighting Irish, who were on the critical list after going 30-26-1 and appearing in two minor bowl games in Gerry Faust's five years. Not only did he patch, repair and improve, but he won it all!

Holtz has now wakened the echoes of Knute Rockne, The Gipper and the Four Horsemen.

In less than three years, less time than anyone imagined, Holtz had instilled a confidence in players that had them saying, "There's no reason we shouldn't win a national championship." They were right. Three years ago,

See ■ Holtz, ND-4

What's inside:

Phoenix Gazette   Mon. Jan. 2, 1989

A front-page high-five was in order as the Fighting Irish celebrated their eighth AP national crown.

1988 NATIONAL
NOTRE DAME
CHAMPIONS

Officially Licensed Product of Univ. of Notre Dame

Rocket Man

Notre Dame fans in the late 1980s and early '90s thought every opposing punt and kickoff was a Fighting Irish touchdown waiting to happen. After watching Tim Brown dash and dance his way to the 1987 Heisman Trophy, an even more explosive return specialist burst onto the scene in 1988.

Soft-spoken Raghib Ismail arrived in South Bend from Wilkes-Barre, Pennsylvania, with 40-yard dash times measured in the sub-4.3-second range and an extra gear that can't be taught. His first name, pronounced Rah-GIB, did not exactly roll off the tongue, so "Rocket" served as his one-word moniker. And this "Rocket" took off!

Ismail's first big day came against Rice during Notre Dame's 1988 national title season. The freshman receiver returned two kickoffs for touchdowns against the Owls, matching the two TDs he'd scored earlier in the season.

"When he hits the hole," said Rice coach Jerry Berndt, "it's a touchdown."

From there, despite opposing punters and kickers doing all they could to keep the ball out of his hands, Rocket was virtually unstoppable. He returned two kickoffs and a punt for scores and rushed for a pair of touchdowns during an All-American slate in 1989. In 1990, he finished second to BYU quarterback Ty Detmer in the Heisman Trophy race but won Walter Camp Player of the Year honors after rushing for three touchdowns, hauling in

One small crease, and "Rocket" was gone. Ismail set a school-record with five touchdowns on kickoff returns in his Notre Dame career.

Hindsight Is 20/20

On his weekly television show the morning after a 1989 home loss to Notre Dame, Michigan coach Bo Schembechler stated the obvious: He should never have let Raghib Ismail return another ball after the speedster took the third-quarter kickoff 88 yards for a touchdown.

"I would think so," Schembechler replied when asked if he should have kept the ball out of Ismail's hands. "You'd kick away from a guy who just ran one back on you. But we kicked it right to him."

Ismail celebrates his second punt return touchdown of the day during this September 16, 1989, battle against Michigan.

Rocket said he was shocked to see the football again. While he was only grazed by defenders on the first return, he had to break an early tackle attempt on the second one. Once past the first wave of Wolverines, however, Ismail was loose for a 92-yard score. Michigan had not allowed an opponent to return a kickoff for a touchdown since 1957. Two in one game led to a 24–19 Irish victory.

"I really thought we were going to be pretty good in covering kicks," Schembechler said. "Until today."

two scoring passes, and reaching the end zone on a kickoff return for the record fifth time in his career.

Though he left Notre Dame after his junior year for a pro career in Canada and the NFL—a decision he admits regretting—Rocket kept his promise to his mother by returning to South Bend and earning his degree in American Studies in 1994.

The "Phantom" Clip

A wild celebration went for naught after Ricky Watters (top), Raghib Ismail (bottom), and their Irish teammates looked back to see a yellow flag on the field during the Orange Bowl on January 1, 1991.

Ninety-one yards that do not appear anywhere on Raghib "Rocket" Ismail's official stats were among the most memorable of his Notre Dame career. The setting: the Orange Bowl in Miami, Florida, on New Year's Day 1991. The opponent: No. 1-ranked Colorado, seeking its first national championship.

The hold-your-breath moment: Colorado, leading 10–9 and punting from near midfield with 43 seconds remaining, put the ball in Ismail's hands at the nine-yard line instead of booting it out of bounds. NBC's Dick Enberg provided this call:

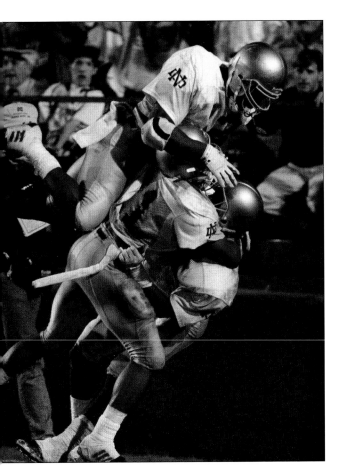

"The Rocket... he's corralled for a moment, breaks into the clear. One man to beat... and he won't get him! The Rocket Ismail has done it again! Touchdown, Notre Dame!"

Were that the end of it, the final play of Ismail's college career would have ranked among the most legendary plays in Notre Dame football history. Some might argue that it still belongs there.

Ismail shook loose a Colorado defender who appeared to have a sure tackle, then brushed off two less promising attempts to stop him and easily outraced the punter down the right sideline. Teammate Ricky Watters came flying toward Ismail in the end zone, flattening him in celebration while yelling, "I love you, man! I love you!"

Then the stadium announcer interrupted: "There is a flag on the play."

"I was laying on the ground," recalled Ismail, "and Ricky Watters took his gaze from me and literally said, 'Nooooooo!'"

Announced Enberg to his national TV audience: "There is a flag down at the Notre Dame 37, so hold on. A sensational individual effort by Raghib 'The Rocket' Ismail...91 yards, but will it count?"

It would not. Back in Notre Dame territory, senior defensive back Greg Davis had blocked Colorado's Tim James from a side angle. One official ruled it was a block in the back, calling a 15-yard clipping penalty. Davis pleaded that it was a legal play, insisting his head was in front of James when he made the block.

Colorado fans see the replay one way; Notre Dame fans another. What most agree on is that James would not have brought down the Rocket, even if he had been left untouched.

The Buffaloes escaped with a national title. Notre Dame finished 9–3. It was the last time Ismail touched the ball during a three-year career in which his dazzling skills led the Irish to a 33–4 record.

And though the final 91 yards blazed by the incomparable Rocket did not count, they were pure magic.

The Snow Bowl

The "Snow Bowl" neither adequately describes the weather encountered by Penn State and Notre Dame on November 14, 1992, nor quite does justice to the battle staged in South Bend that afternoon.

It rained, snowed, sleeted, and even briefly turned sunny, all in a bitter span of three-and-a-half hours. And when Reggie Brooks stretched out to catch the winning two-point conversion pass from Rick Mirer with a blanket of snow covering much of the field and 20 seconds on the clock, the game was destined to be a classic.

Snow and frigid temperatures were nothing new to Nittany Lions–Fighting Irish clashes. The 1987 game in Happy Valley featured windchills well below zero, and one could practically forecast snow in South Bend by an appearance from Penn State in the late 1980s. Kickoff temperature was 32 degrees on this day, with wet snow falling. The pace of the flurries picked up several times, which made the sun's second-half cameo even more shocking.

By then, defense and slick conditions had set the tone. The Irish had just three field goals. Penn State found the end zone early, but star Notre Dame freshman Bobby Taylor blocked the extra point. It was tied 9–9 before the Lions took advantage of an Irish fumble, completing a short touchdown drive for a 16–9 lead with 4:25 to play.

Mirer, Brooks, Jerome Bettis, Aaron Taylor, Irv Smith, Craig Hentrich, and their senior classmates were playing their final home game. "We had one shot," Mirer recalled years later, "and that was it."

Mirer's 21-yard pass to Bettis, 15-yard scramble, and 17-yard pass to Ray Griggs helped Notre Dame march

Despite the best efforts of the grounds crew to keep the yard lines visible, the 1992 Notre Dame–Penn State game might as well have been played on an ice rink.

inside Penn State's ten-yard line. Facing fourth-and-goal from the three-yard line with 25 seconds on the clock, Mirer found Bettis in the end zone. Touchdown, Notre Dame.

In those days, overtime was not an option, so the Irish decided to go for two points and the win. Holtz drew up a four-option pass play from an empty-backfield set. Option No. 4 was Brooks.

With loads of time but his first three receivers covered, Mirer rolled to his right and saw his 5'8" tailback racing toward the right corner of the end zone. Mirer floated the ball toward the back corner. Brooks stretched, pulled it in, and tucked it to his chest just before hitting the cold ground. Fans and teammates pinned him in celebration of a 17–16 triumph—one of the most memorable in Notre Dame Stadium history.

1992 Sugar Bowl

In December 1991, a waiter approached Lou Holtz as he and his family dined at an Orlando, Florida, restaurant, a few days before his underdog Irish battled Florida in the Sugar Bowl in New Orleans. "Let me ask you a question," the young man asked the famed coach.

"What's the difference between Notre Dame and Cheerios?"

Holtz played along, pretending he didn't know what was coming.

"Cheerios *belong* in a bowl," the waiter said. The punch line might have drawn laughter—and agreement—among Florida fans but not at this table. Indeed, the 10–1 Gators were expected to race past 9–3 Notre Dame with relative ease. Their speed, the experts felt, and head coach Steve Spurrier's high-scoring offense would be too much for the Irish. Florida was the SEC champion and had swept eight straight games, the latest a victory over powerful Florida State. The Gators were ranked third in the nation; the Irish No. 18.

Holtz relayed the Cheerios line to his players before the Sugar Bowl, of course, and Notre Dame performed like a team determined to prove it did, indeed, belong.

It was not Florida's speed that dominated but the power of Irish running back Jerome Bettis. "The Bus"

ran 16 times for 150 yards and three scores in a 39–28 Irish win, while teammates Rodney Culver and Tony Brooks rushed for 96 and 68 yards, respectively.

Florida moved the ball, too. The teams combined for 944 yards of offense and set a Sugar Bowl record for points. However, the Gators squandered points on six trips to or inside the Notre Dame 20-yard line, kicking five field goals. Irish defenders flew to the football when it mattered the most.

"We had a chance to score 50 points, but we didn't do it," Spurrier noted.

Bettis, a battering ram listed in the program at 5'11" and 247 pounds, put the Irish ahead for good 25–22 when he slammed in from three yards out with 4:48 left in the game. Then, after a fourth-down Shane Matthews pass was dropped at the Notre Dame 30-yard line, Bettis put the game away with a 49-yard touchdown dash.

"Everybody said we didn't deserve to be here," Holtz said. "But we're holding our heads high right now because we beat a fine, fine football team."

Later, he allowed himself to think that somewhere, a waiter might be crying in his Cheerios. It was a better finish than even the comeback Holtz delivered that night in the restaurant.

"It's my turn to ask you a question," Holtz told the waiter. "What's the difference between Lou Holtz and a golf pro?" The waiter shrugged. The coach quipped, "Golf pros give tips; Lou Holtz won't."

A trophy that many figured was destined for Gainesville, Florida, instead wound up in South Bend after Notre Dame's 39–28 upset of the Florida Gators in the 1992 Sugar Bowl.

During the 1992 Sugar Bowl, Irish running back Jerome Bettis carried just 16 times, but he averaged nearly ten yards per rush and put the game out of reach in the fourth quarter.

ND–Florida State 1993

Florida State coach Bobby Bowden tried to downplay Notre Dame's mystique and tradition entering a 1993 date with the Irish, and his players took his words to heart. They arrived in South Bend with the swagger of a No. 1-ranked team that had won 16 consecutive games—a team that had lost just once to a school outside its home state since 1989. The Seminoles wore green and gold baseball caps with shamrocks. Wide receiver Kez McCorvey called Notre Dame's most famous coach "Rock Knutne."

Though it was a battle between the nation's two top-rated teams, Florida State was a two-touchdown favorite in some circles. "People have said that we might be one of the best college football teams in history," FSU's Matt Frier noted.

On this day—an overcast, 59-degree, mid-November afternoon—Notre Dame was better.

Pounding the smaller, faster visitors with a punishing ground game while mixing in enough big passes to keep the chains moving, the Irish overcame a 7–0 deficit with 24 consecutive points for a wide third-quarter cushion. They led 31–17 with 6:53 left before the Seminoles staged a late rally. When cornerback Shawn Wooden knocked down a Charlie Ward pass in the end zone as time expired, the Irish had seized an unlikely position in the driver's seat of the national championship race.

Notre Dame averaged 5.2 yards per play and rushed for four scores against a defense that had allowed just two rushing touchdowns in its previous nine games combined. Lee Becton carried 26 times for 122 yards and a score.

Some, including Matthews Grid Ratings and the National Championship Foundation, considered the Fighting Irish national champions in 1993 based on a head-to-head win over Florida State, whom the AP crowned national champs.

The Ultimate Letdown

It was a total buzz kill. After their monumental upset of Florida State in 1993, all the top-ranked and unbeaten Fighting Irish had to do to assure themselves a shot at the national title was defeat the unheralded visitors from Boston College a week later.

However, this edition of college football's Catholic "Holy War" left Irish fans looking to the heavens for answers after Boston College's David Gordon kicked a last-second, career-long, 41-yard field goal for a 41–39 victory.

The Golden Eagles, 7–2 entering the game, squandered a 38–17 fourth-quarter lead before driving for the winning points in the final 1:09. Gordon's kick turned what looked like a historic Irish comeback into a historic flop.

Notre Dame bounced back to top Texas A&M 24–21 in the Cotton Bowl. With the Irish and Florida State each owning one loss and Notre Dame having won the head-to-head battle, some in blue and gold lobbied for national title consideration.

The pollsters were not swayed by the argument. Florida State was crowned national champion. Notre Dame finished No. 2. It was controversial, to say the least.

In 1993, a stunning loss to Boston College forced Notre Dame to settle for a Cotton Bowl date with Texas A&M.

"We were No. 2 in the country at the time, but we were a two-touchdown underdog. I thought that was sort of a lack of respect for our program," said Notre Dame coach Lou Holtz, who had invited reporters to his home for dinner two days before the game. Most believed Holtz knew something special was about to happen.

"I did nothing right that week," Bowden lamented. "I tried to downplay their spirit.... But they made us eat everything that was said."

Florida State's vaunted defense was no match for the power-running of Ray Zellars and the Irish in this battle of the unbeatens on November 13, 1993.

What's the Deal with NBC?

Some call NBC the Notre Dame Broadcasting Company. The lucrative deal that has given NBC exclusive broadcasting rights to Notre Dame home football games since 1991 is often one of the first reasons Irish bashers list for rooting against the blue and gold. While Notre Dame profits handsomely from its NBC pact, other Division I schools *share* network and cable TV revenues under College Football Association contracts—making those contracts even less valuable when Notre Dame decided to go its own way.

Long known for tradition, Notre Dame welcomed a change to the scoreboard in the early 1990s when NBC Sports signed on to carry all Fighting Irish home games.

Sports Illustrated reported the original five-year contract under the headline, "We're Notre Dame and You're Not." That first deal paid the university approximately $7 million per home game. Three subsequent five-year contracts have been signed. The most recent one, which began in 2006, runs through the 2010 season and generates roughly $9 million per home game.

Notre Dame uses much of the revenue for its nonathletic, undergraduate scholarships. In late 2003, the school reported that 1,263 undergraduates had received more than $12.6 million in aid from this endowment, while $5.5 million from the NBC revenues had gone to doctoral fellowships and $4 million to MBA scholarships.

"While our partnership with NBC has been important to Irish athletics," offered former Notre Dame president Edward "Monk" Malloy, "it is the general student body that has been the greatest beneficiary."

If Notre Dame has filled its coffers with the exclusive contract, some have wondered whether NBC might be quietly kicking itself over the price. Certainly, ratings would be higher had the Irish maintained a winning pace. In the first three years of the deal, Notre Dame went 31–5–1 and won three straight bowl games. Since then, the Irish are 101–67–1 and have gone winless in nine bowl appearances.

Saturday Night Live, the late-night NBC comedy, parodied the network's commitment to Notre Dame football in a 2007 bit. A spoof commercial promoted NBC's willingness to pay top dollar to broadcast one bumbling team instead of airing top 25 matchups like other networks do. It ended, "Touchdown, other guys!"

NBC Universal Sports & Olympics chairman Dick Ebersol contends that the deal remains prized by the network.

"We are delighted to be continuing our landmark agreement with Notre Dame, which remains the most powerful brand in college sports," said Ebersol. "We covet our association with Notre Dame because of its storied tradition, exceptional values, and commitment to excellence, both on and off the field."

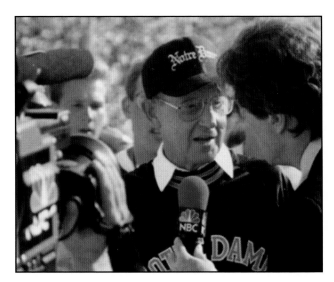

Sideline reporter John Dockery became quite familiar with Irish coach Lou Holtz after NBC started carrying all the action.

Stadium Expansion

You can't please everyone. Even though expansion of Notre Dame Stadium in the 1990s allowed more than 21,000 extra fans to witness each home game and doubled locker-room space in the "House that Rockne Built," at least one regular refused to call the changes "progress."

"One usher quit," Russell Gagnon, director of stadium personnel, told *The Observer* in 2001. "He said Knute Rockne designed it, and we've made it different, and he didn't want to work here anymore."

Rockne was a visionary. He designed the stadium, which opened in 1930, to hold between 50,000 and 60,000 at a time when college football crowds of even 20,000 were considered large. Given the demand for Notre Dame football tickets in the modern era, most agree that Rockne would have demanded an upgrade.

After the usual sellout gathering of 59,075 watched the last home game of the 1996 season, Notre Dame Stadium opened to 80,225 in 1997. The difference cost $50 million and required 21 months to complete (the project began in 1995). It included an upper seating area around the stadium, two new scoreboards, a three-tiered press box, a new natural-grass field and drainage system, more concession areas and restrooms, and other upgrades as well. The capacity, modified to 80,795 in 2001, put Notre Dame Stadium among the ten largest in the country at the time.

One of the more popular aspects of the renovation was not the new but the old. The original brick exterior of the stadium remains the inner wall of the main concourse, with the bulk of the expansion having gone up around it. While meeting the need for growth and progress, the past was preserved, and the special, intimate feel of a Fighting Irish football game was kept intact.

Notre Dame Stadium, shown here in 1996, was about to welcome more than 20,000 extra fans through the gates for each home game beginning the following season.

Stadium Expansion Facts

Did you know?

- As of the end of the 2007 season, Notre Dame has sold out 199 consecutive home games. Since a 1973 Thanksgiving Day game against Air Force, when there were a few empty seats, every Irish home game has been a sellout.

- Approximately 240,000 concrete blocks, 700,000 bricks, and 500 cubic yards of mortar were used in Notre Dame Stadium's 1995–96 renovation.

- More than 3,500 sheets of drawings were used in the design for the 1995–96 renovation.

- Eleven new openings were cut in the old stadium's brick exterior to connect the old and new lower concourse areas.

Notre Dame tradition has been built on great players and coaches, famous landmarks, Heisman trophies, and national championships.

An 1885 diploma signed by Father Sorin does not look much different than the degrees earned today by those who survive the rigors of a Notre Dame education.

A football card celebrates Raghib Ismail's 1990 Walter Camp Player of the Year Award.

The AFCA's Academic Achievement Award is a regular in the trophy case of Notre Dame, a school that emphasizes classroom excellence.

Key chains, buttons, magnets, medals, and ribbons—if you want a Fighting Irish trinket, you won't have trouble finding one in South Bend.

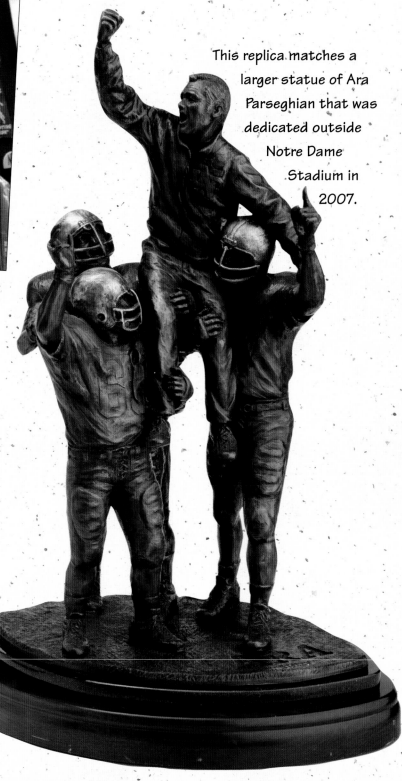

This replica matches a larger statue of Ara Parseghian that was dedicated outside Notre Dame Stadium in 2007.

This poster from 1987 celebrates the 100th anniversary of Notre Dame football.

Independent Status

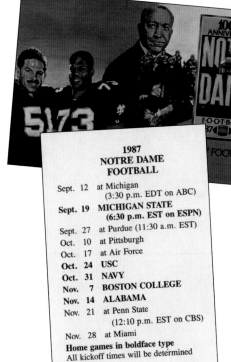

**1987
NOTRE DAME
FOOTBALL**

Sept. 12 at Michigan
(3:30 p.m. EDT on ABC)
Sept. 19 MICHIGAN STATE
(6:30 p.m. EST on ESPN)
Sept. 27 at Purdue (11:30 a.m. EST)
Oct. 10 at Pittsburgh
Oct. 17 at Air Force
Oct. 24 USC
Oct. 31 NAVY
Nov. 7 BOSTON COLLEGE
Nov. 14 ALABAMA
Nov. 21 at Penn State
(12:10 p.m. EST on CBS)
Nov. 28 at Miami
Home games in boldface type
All kickoff times will be determined
by television

Back in Knute Rockne's day, it was Notre Dame knocking on the Big Ten Conference door, only to be turned away. The roles reversed in the late 1990s when the Big Ten, having added an 11th school in Penn State, had serious talks with Notre Dame about bumping the league's membership to an even dozen.

By then, Notre Dame's status as a football independent had become something of a sacred trust between the school and many of its supporters. It came as no surprise that Notre Dame, after some consideration, said no to the Big Ten. Even when Irish athletics joined the Big East Conference in 1994, it almost went without saying that the deal did not include football membership.

"I've talked to Notre Dame so much that if you gave me a dollar for every time I've talked to them about being a part of our [football] league, I could probably retire," Big East commissioner Mike Tranghese said. "But Notre Dame has said consistently that they put a high degree of importance on being a football independent."

Tradition, scheduling, and, of course, money factor into the equation any time Notre Dame ponders life in a football conference. And not necessarily in that order. Its independent status has certainly contributed to Irish

tradition. Notre Dame was the first major school willing to travel coast to coast to take on all comers. Today, the Irish have little trouble finding interested opponents, and their independent status allows them to maintain rivalries with the likes of Michigan, Southern Cal, and Navy.

Financially, independence is a big victory for Notre Dame. Unlike conference teams, the Irish are not required to share bowl game and television revenue with other schools. Given their exclusive television contract with NBC, that amounts to a multimillion-dollar advantage, in addition to the edge in exposure the Irish gain by having all their home games and virtually all their road contests available to a national audience.

"Notre Dame has a distinct identity that is the product of more than a century and a half of institutional independence," explained then-president Father Edward Malloy in turning down the Big Ten in 1999. "As a Catholic university with a national constituency, we believe independence continues to be our best way forward, not just in athletics but, first and foremost, in fulfillment of our academic aspirations."

1988 NOTRE DAME FOOTBALL			
Date	Opponent	Site	*Time
Sept. 10	**MICHIGAN**	**NOTRE DAME**	8:00 EST/CDT
Sept. 17	Michigan State	East Lansing	12:00 EDT
Sept. 24	**PURDUE**	**NOTRE DAME**	12:20 EST/CDT
Oct. 1	**STANFORD**	**NOTRE DAME**	6:00 EST/CDT
Oct. 8	Pittsburgh	Pittsburgh	7:00 EDT
Oct. 15	**MIAMI**	**NOTRE DAME**	1:30 EST/CDT
Oct. 22	**AIR FORCE**	**NOTRE DAME**	12:20 EST/CDT
Oct. 29	Navy	Baltimore	12:10 EDT
Nov. 5	**RICE**	**NOTRE DAME**	12:20 EST
Nov. 19	**PENN STATE**	**NOTRE DAME**	12:00 EST
Nov. 26	USC	Los Angeles	12:30 PST

*All times are tentative and subject to change due to television
Pictured on front are '88 Tri-captains—Ned Bolcar, Mark Green, and Andy Heck

Its independent status allows Notre Dame to schedule rivals like Michigan, USC, and Navy on a regular basis.

Some, including the Big Ten, have pursued the Fighting Irish football program for inclusion in a conference but to no avail.

The Bob Davie Years

Bob Davie's first outing as head coach at the University of Notre Dame was played at the newly expanded stadium before 80,225 fans—more people than had ever witnessed a game in South Bend. It was fitting because for most of his five-year tour as head coach, Davie felt his share of eyes on him, always evaluating, sometimes celebrating, and frequently second-guessing his every move.

That's life as Notre Dame's football boss. Davie accepted it when he ascended from his defensive coordinator position to replace Lou Holtz in 1997. He had no previous head-coaching experience but was respected for his defensive success at Notre Dame and Texas A&M. He inherited a team that began 1997 ranked 11th in the nation.

To call the Davie era a roller-coaster ride would be an understatement. Coach Davie won his opener against Georgia Tech 17–13 but followed with four straight losses. He was the first rookie coach in school history to take his first team to a bowl game—a 27–9 loss to LSU that ended a 7–6 campaign. Davie's 1998 team started 9–1 before dropping back-to-back games to end the season, and what followed was a 5–7 slumber in 1999.

Even sharper twists and turns followed. Arnaz Battle, Julius Jones, and the Fighting Irish beat Texas A&M and nearly knocked off top-ranked Nebraska in the first two games of 2000, falling 27–24 in overtime against the Cornhuskers. They won their last seven games of the

Bob Davie was a respected defensive boss, but he was unable to carry on the momentum of his predecessor, Lou Holtz, once taking over the head-coaching job in 1997.

regular season to finish 9–2, and Davie was rewarded with a five-year contract extension before a Fiesta Bowl date with Oregon State.

But the Irish were dismantled 41–9 in that game and then lost their first three games of 2001 as the pressure on Davie mounted. After a 5–6 slate marked his second losing season in five years, Davie became the first Notre Dame coach ever fired with time left on his contract.

The O'Leary Fiasco

If Notre Dame fans felt their program had reached a new low with losing records in two of Bob Davie's final three seasons, all they could do was shake their heads after the hiring of Davie's replacement.

George O'Leary was named Irish head coach on December 9, 2001. Four days later, after inconsistencies on his résumé were exposed, O'Leary resigned.

O'Leary's résumé claimed he had earned a master's degree from New York University, which was untrue. It also overstated his playing career at his alma mater, the University of New Hampshire.

"Due to a selfish and thoughtless act many years ago, I have personally embarrassed Notre Dame, its alumni, and fans," O'Leary said in a statement announcing his resignation.

While late-night talk show hosts and Notre Dame bashers across the country had a field day with the news, it was back to the drawing board for the Fighting Irish.

By George, these T-shirts went in and out of style in a hurry.

by it's **GEORGE** O'**LEARY**

HEAD COACH
UNIVERSITY OF NOTRE DAME
DECEMBER 9, 2001

"In Ty We Trust"

He was Notre Dame's first African American head coach in any sport. Ty Willingham, a hard-working former Michigan State football walk-on, took over the most storied college football team in America in 2002 and promptly won his first eight games, attaining a No. 4 national ranking. Students wore "In Ty We Trust" T-shirts, celebrating the man who became the first in Irish history to win ten games in his rookie year—a refreshing turnaround from a 5–6 effort under Bob Davie in 2001.

Then, just as quickly as Willingham burst onto the scene to win multiple Coach of the Year honors with his 10–3 debut in 2002, he fell out of favor for an inability to maintain that winning momentum.

Facing a powerhouse schedule with a freshman quarterback named Brady Quinn in 2003, Notre Dame lost six of its first eight games, including a 37–0 thrashing at the hands of Florida State, the second-worst home loss in Irish history at the time. Willingham's second-year ledger was 5–7.

Although the following year's 6–5 record qualified the Irish for a date with Oregon State at the Insight Bowl, speculation was rampant that Notre Dame would fire Willingham less than three years into his

five-year deal—a break from the school tradition of honoring initial contracts through their completion.

"At the end of the day, we simply have not made the progress on the field that we need to make," said then-athletic director Kevin White, noting that Willingham handled himself with great integrity and that the program's academic performance had never been better. Willingham was fired before the team's 38–21 bowl loss.

"My goals have always been to inspire people to be the best they could be, on and off the field," Willingham said after learning of his firing, noting that his 21–15 record was a bigger disappointment to himself than it was to Notre Dame. "I believe that I have been true to that in my time here at Notre Dame."

Ty Willingham was the first coach in Irish history to win ten games in his first season.

From the Stands to the Sideline

As a Notre Dame student, Charlie Weis smiled for his yearbook photo and cheered the 1977 Irish to the national title.

A Bill Parcells disciple, Weis does not mince words when expressing his high expectations.

The first man in history to go from the student section seats of Notre Dame Stadium to the most prominent place on the sideline, Charlie Weis brought to the head-coaching position in 2005 something of great value to administrators, alumni, and fans longing for success—a deep loyalty to the university and its rich football history.

Weis was a Flanner Hall roommate of former Fighting Irish running back Terry Eurick. He cheered Notre Dame to a national championship in 1977, his senior year. He lived and died with Irish football for four years and beyond. Now, the stakes are higher.

"If somebody came along 20, 30 years ago and told me: 'You're going to be the head coach at Notre Dame,' I'd have told them they were hallucinating," Weis told *Notre Dame Magazine* in 2005.

Between his last time exiting the stadium as a student and his first time charging through the tunnel as coach, Weis built an impressive résumé as an offensive mastermind. He earned a Super Bowl championship with the New York Giants in 1990 as an assistant to Bill Parcells and three more as offensive coordinator for Bill Belichick's New England Patriots between 2000 and 2004.

Charlie Weis's Hannah & Friends Foundation

Charlie Weis calls his daughter, Hannah, his "guiding angel." His wife, Maura, uses the phrase *different abilities* instead of *disabilities*.

When she was pregnant in 1995, Maura was told that her unborn daughter Hannah had polycystic kidney disease and might not live beyond a few days. She was later diagnosed with pervasive developmental disorder (PDD), a disease similar to autism. More than a dozen years later, she is still enriching lives. Maura calls her "100 percent perfect."

In 2003, Charlie and Maura started Hannah & Friends, a foundation that raises money for people with special needs. Gold-colored bracelets sold in the Notre Dame bookstore and elsewhere contribute to the cause.

Bracelet sales have been swift in support of Weis's Hannah & Friends foundation.

Weis does not hesitate to wear his Super Bowl rings while on the recruiting trail. The New Jersey native will take any edge he can get. If a prospective recruit discounts the mystique and tradition of Notre Dame football, however, Weis would rather look elsewhere.

"I have a passion for Notre Dame," Weis noted. "Recruiting is selling. Having gone to Notre Dame, it's an easier sell for me than it would be for somebody who hasn't been to Notre Dame. . . . I'd rather not have a kid come here than say a bunch of things he wants to hear."

Weis took his first two Irish teams to major bowl games—the Fiesta Bowl in 2005 and the Sugar Bowl in 2006. He would be the first to say that Notre Dame tradition demands better. It demands championships.

All-Americans of the Era

Tim Brown won Notre Dame's seventh Heisman Trophy, and Rocket Ismail took flight as Lou Holtz revived football fortunes in South Bend in the late 1980s. Brady Quinn and Jeff Samardzija rewrote the passing and receiving record books as Charlie Weis attempted to do the same in the 21st century.

In between, there were many players who took their places among the Irish greats with All-American performances. Here's a look at some of those players.

Andy Heck, Tackle/Tight End (1985–88): A tight end in his first three years, Heck switched to tackle during spring practice before his senior season in 1988. That year,

Chris Zorich (50) was not the biggest man in the middle of the Irish defense, but his high energy routinely disrupted the opposition.

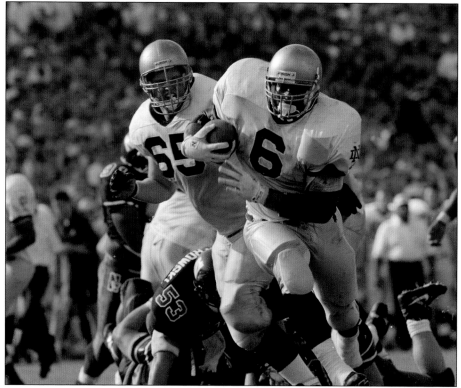

he cocaptained the Fighting Irish to a 12–0 record and a national championship.

Michael Stonebreaker, Linebacker (1986–90): Blessed with one of the great names in Notre Dame football history, Stonebreaker delivered hits to match the moniker. He was a ball carrier's nightmare during two first-team All-American seasons in 1988 and 1990.

Todd Lyght, Cornerback (1987–90): Before becoming one of the best cover corners in the NFL, Lyght anchored a talented Irish secondary that won a national championship in 1988. The three-year starter racked up 11 career interceptions.

The bruising Jerome Bettis (6) ran over, around, and through defenses as Notre Dame's leading ground-gainer in 1991.

Aaron Taylor earned first-team All-American honors at two different positions and won the Lombardi Award in 1993.

Chris Zorich, Defensive Tackle (1988–90): Some said Zorich was too small to play nose tackle, but his heart and his motor were oversized. The Chicagoan started as a sophomore on the 1988 national title team and won the 1990 Lombardi Award.

Rick Mirer, Quarterback (1989–92): Mirer set a then-school record with 41 career touchdown passes in three years as a starter. He finished second on the school charts in total offense, completions, and passing yards and compiled a sterling 29–7–1 record.

Jerome Bettis, Running Back (1990–92): "The Bus" drove Notre Dame's offense straight down the field, running through tacklers and around them. He averaged 5.7 yards per carry, rushing for 1,912 Irish yards before launching an All-Pro NFL career.

Aaron Taylor, Guard/Tackle (1990–93): A consensus All-American as a junior, offensive guard Taylor switched

to tackle for his senior season and fared even better, winning All-American honors and the 1993 Lombardi Award. He started his final 30 college games.

Shane Walton, Cornerback (1999–02): Walton started his career as an Irish soccer standout but finished it a two-time football All-American and leader of the Irish defense. He was the team MVP for his senior season, when he intercepted seven passes.

Tom Zbikowski, Safety (2004–07): A Golden Gloves amateur boxer, "Zibby" packed a punch in the secondary and on special teams. This fearless competitor scored touchdowns on punt returns, interception returns, and fumble returns.

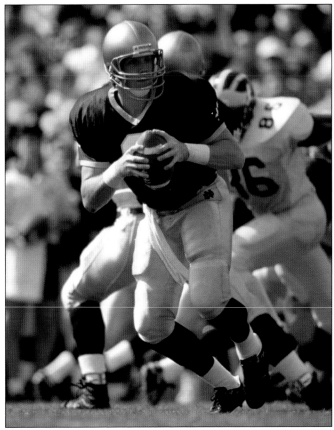

In 1992, Rick Mirer, who grew up in nearby Goshen, Indiana, finished his career as Notre Dame's all-time leader in touchdown passes.

Notre Dame's jerseys have evolved over the years. This 21st-century model features blue, gold, and a green shamrock.

Through good seasons and bad, Notre Dame fans remain true to their school and its colors.

Look magazine presented a sleek Grantland Rice Award to Notre Dame's 1966 national championship team.

THE
Grantland Rice
AWARD

NATIONAL COLLEGIATE FOOTBALL CHAMPIONS
1966
NOTRE DAME
Selected by the Football Writers Association of America
PRESENTED BY
LOOK MAGAZINE

Mobil
Cotton Bowl
Classic
19   94
FIELD SCOVELL TROPHY

The Irish had hoped for a 1993 national title but instead settled for a victory in the Cotton Bowl on January 1, 1994.

Wheaties, the "Breakfast of Champions," showcased the "school of champions" on a cereal box that displayed Notre Dame's expanded stadium.

Former Notre Dame player, coach, and athletic director Elmer Layden was inducted into the Rose Bowl Hall of Fame in 1992.

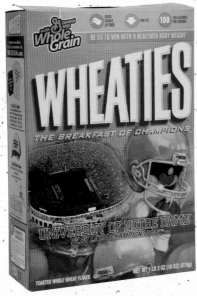

Notre Dame received this trophy when the UPI awarded them the national championship in 1966.

Notre Dame kicked Texas 24–11 to earn 1973 Cotton Bowl hardware.

This page from the January 1, 1995, Fiesta Bowl program takes a look back on Notre Dame's 1994 season, including the tale of freshman quarterback Ron Powlus and a 6–5–1 success rate.

Crushed by the Bush Push

It was perhaps the greatest game Notre Dame ever lost. Not the greatest loss, Fighting Irish fans will insist. There's no such thing as a great loss, or even a good one, at a school where winning is expected and success is measured in national titles.

But no one who witnessed Southern Cal's epic 34–31 escape from Notre Dame Stadium on October 15, 2005, will argue against its inclusion among college football's true classics.

"It was a heck of a game," Irish coach Charlie Weis said two years after the loss. "You knew that you had been part of something special."

In his first season as head coach, Weis had Notre Dame fans celebrating a 4–1 start, a No. 9 national ranking, a Joe Montana appearance at the Friday night pep rally, and a rebirth of the green jerseys. Still, most felt the Irish would be out of their league against the top-ranked Trojans, who were defending national champs and winners of 27 straight games.

In their most inspired effort of the Weis era, the Fighting Irish proved those doubters wrong. Tom Zbikowski's 60-yard punt return in the second quarter gave Notre Dame its first lead, 21–14. The Irish grabbed two more leads in the final period, the second when quarterback Brady Quinn stretched the ball across the goal line with 2:02 remaining.

Notre Dame Stadium was buzzing over the 31–28 margin. The roar could be heard from miles away as the Trojans began a final drive from their own 25-yard line.

"You could never be in a stadium of 80,000 or whatever they hold," noted USC coach Pete Carroll, "and it be louder and more challenging."

The Trojans proved equal to the challenge—and admittedly somewhat fortunate—on two plays that will forever haunt Fighting Irish fans.

The crowd anticipated an Irish victory as USC quarterback Matt Leinart took a fourth-and-nine snap in Notre Dame territory. Leinart threw the ball toward the sideline, where receiver Dwayne Jarrett made a clutch grab and turned it into a 61-yard gain.

After a Leinart fumble popped out of bounds and the game clock mistakenly expired, sending Irish players and fans onto the field in celebration, USC lined up for one more play from the one-yard line—a play that will forever be known as the "Bush Push."

Running back Reggie Bush, who would go on to win the 2005 Heisman Trophy, shoved 2004 Heisman winner Leinart over the goal line on a quarterback sneak for the winning touchdown. "I used all 200 pounds of my body to push Matt in," Bush said.

For the Irish and their fans, who were sitting in stunned silence, it felt like 200 tons of heartache.

Tom Zbikowski (9) put Notre Dame ahead for the first time on an amazing 60-yard punt return for a second-quarter touchdown against Southern Cal.

Cover Boy Brady Quinn

Brady Quinn was many things to many people in his four years at Notre Dame: Boy wonder, in many instances; whipping boy, after the arrival of Coach Charlie Weis; cover boy, for both sports magazines and those trying to appeal to a female audience.

The Notre Dame record book is perfectly clear in its definition of Quinn as one of the best in school history. By the time he was selected by the Cleveland Browns in the 2007 NFL draft, the Columbus, Ohio, native held 36 different school marks, including career completions and yardage, touchdown passes, and lowest interception rate.

Quinn's journey to that lofty position was not an easy one. Under Ty Willingham, the coach who recruited him, he threw 25 interceptions and 26 touchdown passes as a freshman and sophomore and was unable to lead the Irish to a winning ledger.

While the arrival of Weis—who had tutored quarterback Tom Brady with the New England Patriots—brought life to the Irish offense, it also initially brought nightmares to Quinn. Weis was more abrasive with his quarterback than with any other player, pressuring Quinn's practices to the point where game days seemed like a breeze.

The strategy paid dividends.

"Because he has been able to handle a lot," Weis said before the 2006 season, Quinn's senior year, "we've been able to do a lot."

Brady Quinn set Notre Dame career records for completions, passing yards, touchdown passes, and total offense, among others. He was responsible for 606 career points—256 more than his closest competition, Rick Mirer.

Quinn, 6'3" and a chiseled 235 pounds, put in countless hours of work on the practice field and in the weight room over his final two seasons. He led the Irish to a 19–6 record in 2005 and 2006, firing 69 touchdown passes against just 14 interceptions during that span. He won the 2006 Unitas Award as the nation's best senior quarterback.

"Hopefully, with what I've done over the last four years," Quinn said before his final game, "I'd like to be remembered as the quarterback who helped Notre Dame go from a time when we weren't doing so well and helped turn the program around."

Jeff Samardzija, aka "The Shark"

It was never difficult to spot Brady Quinn's favorite target. Look for the guy with shoulder-length hair flowing out from the back of his helmet—the guy with the long stride and sure hands—the guy with the million-dollar pitching arm that eventually convinced him to bypass an NFL career and pursue his dream of playing major league baseball.

Jeff Samardzija was that man. For Quinn, he was *the* man.

The Indiana native set single-season school records for receiving yards (1,249) and touchdown catches (15) as a junior in 2005. After signing with the Chicago Cubs and pitching in the minor leagues during the summer of 2006, he returned to Notre Dame for his senior season and became the school's career leader in receiving yards (2,593).

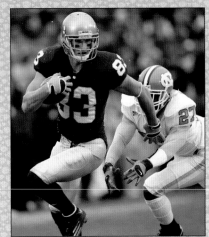

Jeff Samardzija caught 27 career touchdown passes, which set a school record.

Game Day

There's nothing quite like a Notre Dame home football weekend. Fighting Irish fans are biased in that view, of course, but millions with no allegiance to the school have discovered the same magic over the years.

"I wanted to belong," Kieran Darcy, a member of the latter group, wrote for ESPN.com after watching 80,000 fans salute the Irish players, helmets raised, following a 2003 *loss* to Michigan State. "It wasn't exactly that moment when Rudy was carried triumphantly off the field. It was even better."

Whether a first-time pilgrim like Darcy or a veteran of home weekends on Notre Dame's picturesque campus, there are countless sights to see, traditions to soak up, and tips to keep in mind.

Book Early: Hotels anywhere near South Bend sell out more than a year in advance for home football weekends. For a game early in the fall, consider camping. Or plan to stay down the Indiana Toll Road in La Porte or Valparaiso.

Friday Is Kickoff: Why wait for Saturday? Notre Dame hosts a Kickoff Luncheon (formerly the Quarterback Club Luncheon) in the Joyce Center—across the street from the stadium—every home game Friday at noon. And Friday night pep rallies at the same venue are a sight to behold. Your ears might not thank you, though. Tickets for both should be ordered in advance. Check und.cstv.com, the official Web site.

Irish Eyes Are Smiling: Look around while tailgating Saturday morning. Try to find someone who isn't smiling. From bagpipe music to rock 'n' roll, cheap hot dogs to gourmet spreads, impromptu games of football to beanbag tossing, the celebration starts long before kickoff.

Where's the Beef?: Stop for a steak sandwich at the Knights of Columbus Hall on South Quad, between the stadium and the Golden Dome. It's more about the tradition than the meat. They've been serving them up for more than 50 years.

Notre Dame's marching band is the oldest college band in continuous existence in the United States.

(Center): The kilt-wearing Irish Guard provides a lead block as the band marches toward the stadium amid cheering fans.

What's a parade without a leprechaun leading the way? It must be a Notre Dame home game.

Cruise Campus: Tour guides take groups around campus, pointing out the rich history and landmarks. The find-it-yourself method works just as well. Light a candle at the Grotto, wear out your camera's battery in Sacred Heart Basilica (no flash photography allowed), and try to frame a photo of the Golden Dome through the leaves of a tree. You'll be sharing one of the prettiest campuses in America with thousands of others who love the place.

Tunnel Vision: Ninety minutes to two hours before kickoff, players emerge from pregame mass at the Basilica to a tunnel of fans that begins forming in the morning hours. They walk to the stadium amid cheers that are reserved for the actual game at other schools.

Strike Up the Band: The marching band performs about 90 minutes before kickoff on the steps of Bond Hall, followed by Irish Guard "inspection," where Guard members stand completely still while fellow students check out their duds, occasionally taunting them and testing their ability to remain stoic. Guard members then lead the band—and a trail of fans—toward the stadium.

Student Teachers: Want to learn how to behave once inside the stadium? Watch the students. They never sit. They belt out "America the Beautiful" and the National Anthem. They hoist, swirl, and wave their arms in a variety of rhythms, following the lead of the band. They dance the Irish jig with their arms around their neighbors. They hoist fellow students in the air for "push-ups" that reflect the number of Notre Dame points on the scoreboard. They jingle their keys before

Irish eyes are smiling as Notre Dame—sporting green jerseys—prepares to do battle against USC on October 15, 2005.

"key" plays. And they shout at the top of their lungs when the opposing team has the ball, truly becoming a "12th player."

Cheerleaders: They practice four nights a week, and the effort shows. The women on the squad generally arrive on campus with cheerleading experience. Few men do, but that doesn't seem to hold them back. Needless to say, the number of interested male candidates has increased since Notre Dame began admitting female students in 1972.

Look Around: Someone—maybe it's you—is seeing the unadorned bluegrass field of Notre Dame Stadium for the first time in a lifetime of cheering for the Irish. And he or she is wearing the look Rudy's father wore in the movie, when he called it "the most beautiful sight these eyes have ever seen."

"Love Thee, Notre Dame": Win or lose, Notre Dame's players and student section salute each other after the game and the band plays. The grand finale is "Notre Dame Our Mother," the alma mater. It begins in reverent tones and builds to a booming crescendo. Students, alumni, and fans sway back and forth in unison with their arms resting on neighboring shoulders. Brace for a few misty eyes.

After each game—win or lose—Irish players salute fans in the student section with raised helmets.

The Voices of Notre Dame

For some, the voice of Notre Dame football will always belong to Lindsey Nelson, the plaid-sportcoat-wearing play-by-play man who called Irish football for 13 years in the 1960s and '70s. "We move to further action," his matter-of-fact delivery would inform a nation of ND fans on condensed replay shows. And the next Irish touchdown drive would begin.

More recently, the honest, midwestern voices of Tony Roberts and Tom Pagna have resonated with fans of the blue and gold.

"I don't think there's a better play-by-play man in the business," said Tom Pagna, a longtime Notre Dame assistant coach who served as Roberts's analyst for 16 years on the Mutual and Westwood One radio networks. "As much as Tony has come to love Notre Dame, he...was completely fair. If the opponent got a raw deal on a call, he was the first one to bring it up. And to me that's the honesty and integrity in the announcing end of it."

Roberts grew up in Chicago rooting *against* Notre Dame. He turned down a chance to call Fighting Irish games in 1979 but jumped into the booth the following year and put his own unique stamp on Saturday afternoons for 26 years. He questioned calls. He spoke his mind. He developed a terrific rapport with Pagna, whom Roberts claims could predict three out of every four Notre Dame plays, and later with former All-American Allen Pinkett, who replaced Pagna as Roberts's sidekick in 2001.

Roberts's voice carries a natural urgency, a gift that keeps listeners leaning toward their radios—and now their computer speakers—in anticipation of the next word. His first Notre Dame game needed no additional energy. It ended on Harry Oliver's last-second, 51-yard field goal to beat Michigan 29–27 in 1980. Eight years later, Roberts called what he considers the greatest game of his era, the 31–30 upset of top-ranked Miami—a game that edged the Irish toward the 1988 national title.

In 2005, Roberts won the College Football Hall of Fame's Chris Schenkel Award, which is given to a broadcaster who has excelled in his field and community. It did not take him long to find a job after Westwood One replaced him the following year with Don Criqui. Roberts reunited with Pagna on Blue and Gold Radio in 2006, treating Internet listeners to analysis and interviews in the tones many Irish fans can hear in their dreams.

A young Lindsey Nelson talks to Hunk Anderson (left) and Marchy Schwartz (right) in the 1930s.

Lindsey Nelson, here interviewing Paul Hornung, was known as much for his wild fashion sense as he was for his turns of phrase.

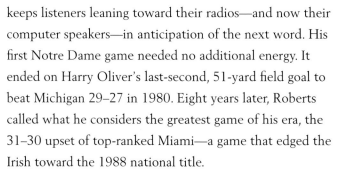

Tony Roberts has been the voice of Notre Dame football since 1980, whether on the radio or via the Internet.

Tom Pagna served as Tony Roberts's sidekick on the radio for 16 years and later wrote several books on the Ara Parseghian years at Notre Dame.

Following the Fighting Irish

Times have changed. So have *Tribunes, Heralds, Observers,* and many other newspaper names in the land.

Notre Dame fans were once highly limited in their methods of following their favorite football team. Aside from listening to the games on the radio or watching them on television, there were few alternatives to reading newspapers from South Bend or Chicago or the handful of decent-size Indiana newspapers that covered the Irish. As recently as the 1980s, calls would flood Notre Dame's student newspaper, *The Observer,* asking about the progress of various players during practices or spring drills.

Now, thanks to the Internet, those calls are more likely to be e-mails, and following the Irish can be an almost full-time passion for anyone so inclined.

Notre Dame's official Web site (www.und.cstv.com) is a great starting point. Fans can watch press conferences, game highlights, and the coach's show, read official news releases, view the media guide, buy merchandise, and order tickets to pep rallies and other home game weekend events. There's even a comprehensive guide to Notre Dame football weekends, with resources for planning a trip to a game.

Those newspapers where Notre Dame coverage has traditionally been strong are now scoured by fans

Notre Dame's official Web site makes use of the increasing interest in Internet video, showing Fighting Irish press conferences and highlights.

from around the world thanks to the Internet. The *South Bend Tribune,* the *Tribune* and *Sun-Times* of Chicago, *The Observer,* and *The Indianapolis Star* are, not surprisingly, among the top producers of Fighting Irish content.

Subscription models such as *Irish Sports Report* and *Blue and Gold Illustrated* are worth considering for those with an unquenchable thirst for all things Irish. Both offer print publications and robust sites for paying subscribers.

"Notre Dame Central" is an indication that NBC Sports doesn't truly go off the air once the helmets are raised toward the student section following Irish home games. The "official network of the Fighting Irish" maintains a Notre Dame Web presence around-the-clock through msnbc.com. Its "Notre Dame Central" section offers articles, video, commentary, and interactive features.

Hunt for yourself. A recent online search for "Notre Dame football" returned more than a million results. There are countless "unofficial" sites and aggregators of Fighting Irish content from other sources, such as blogs, message boards, discussion forums, and fan tributes online.

Imagine what fun marketer and promoter extraordinaire Knute Rockne might have had in the digital age, spreading the word about Notre Dame football and a small Catholic school in the Midwest.

The Observer, Notre Dame's student newspaper, keeps Fighting Irish fans around the world up to speed via the Web.

Notre Dame on the All-Time Charts

Leading Notre Dame has long been considered the summit of the college football coaching profession. The job comes with a different set of expectations than most and a unique set of circumstances: tough admissions standards, a rigorous schedule, and a national spotlight that can rival the glare of the sun.

"Being competitive at Notre Dame meant winning, not coming close," former Fighting Irish coach Lou Holtz noted. "And when the alumni talked about winning, they meant winning them all and winning by large margins."

Those expectations are based on history—a record of winning that can be matched by only one school in college football history.

At the start of the 2008 season, the University of Michigan—the school that taught Notre Dame how to play football in 1887—led all programs in total victories with 869. Notre Dame stood second with 824, while Texas came in third at 820.

For many years Notre Dame led in winning percentage, but Michigan took over the top spot in 2004. Entering the 2006 game between the Irish and Wolverines, Michigan's lead was 0.0006658 of a percent-age point—a margin that would have allowed Notre Dame to regain the lead with a victory. However, the Wolverines prevailed, and the 2007 season only widened the gap. At the start of the 2008 season, Michigan boasted an all-time winning percentage of .7296. Notre Dame was second at .7202.

Still, Notre Dame's 11 consensus national championships, seven Heisman Trophy winners, national visibility, well-known traditions, and demand for excellence on and off the field give Fighting Irish fans ample reason to feel they root for the best program in the land. And no amount of academic standards or difficult scheduling will keep those blue and gold faithful from believing that their team belongs on top of the national landscape.

"Too many people make excuses for the failures of the program," Charlie Weis said shortly after accepting the head-coaching job in 2005. "I'm looking for good kids who can read, write, and play a little football.

"If you're not a good kid, or can't read and write, or can't play, then there's not going to be a place for you at Notre Dame. There are plenty of kids who fit that mold. We're just going to have to do a better job finding them."

Notre Dame football teams have been playing "like a champion" to the tune of 800-plus victories, winning more than seven out of every ten games.

A Dark Cloud Over the Golden Dome: The 2007 Season

The 2007 season was a record setter for Notre Dame's storied football program. These, however, were not the kinds of records the Fighting Irish were chasing. They won three games and lost nine, the most single-season losses in school history. Five of those losses came in their opening five games (another first), which ran their overall losing streak to seven games. A six-game home slump set another school record. And in perhaps the most telling game of the season, the Irish watched their 43-game winning streak against Navy—an NCAA record for consecutive wins by one school over another—dissolve in a 46–44, triple-overtime loss to the visiting Midshipmen.

Yes, it was a bitter fall for Notre Dame coaches, players, and fans alike. And it was made only slightly more respectable when the Irish prevailed in their home finale against Duke and their last game at Stanford to finish the season with back-to-back victories for the first time since 1992.

"Hey, it's still 3–9, let's not kid ourselves," said head coach Charlie Weis, whose first two Irish teams went 9–3 and 10–3 and played in BCS bowl games. "But at least it's 3–9 with two wins at the end of the year."

It was also a 3–9 season that hinged largely on the play of freshmen and sophomores. While seniors such as safety Tom Zbikowski, tight end John Carlson, and defensive lineman Trevor Laws provided leadership, it was a squad comprised primarily of underclassmen that took its lumps

Trevor Laws (98), Bartley Webb (71), and the 2007 Fighting Irish struggled through one of the worst seasons in Notre Dame history.

Jimmy Clausen: The Next Golden QB?

In the 19 months between April 2006, when Jimmy Clausen arrived at the College Football Hall of Fame (in a stretch Hummer limousine) to announce his college choice, until he quarterbacked Notre Dame to back-to-back wins to end his freshman season, the California kid did a lot of growing up.

Now, the "can't-miss kid" who never lost a high school game faces the task of helping the Irish go from 3–9 to national title contenders.

After off-season elbow surgery, Clausen became the first Irish QB in more than 50 years to start his second game as a freshman. He struggled a bit and was replaced midseason. Then, in his final three games, Clausen threw for 636 yards and six touchdowns with just one interception.

Perhaps more importantly, he showed a maturity that led Irish coach Charlie Weis to believe the future is golden indeed.

Jimmy Clausen made his Fighting Irish debut in 2007, and fans are hoping that experience will pave the way to better success in years to come.

in matching 38–0 routs by Michigan and Southern Cal, among other lopsided losses.

Carlson was the lone senior in the season-ending starting offensive lineup. Notre Dame's leading rusher (Robert Hughes), passer (Jimmy Clausen), and receiver (Duval Kamara) in that victory were all freshmen.

"When the going got the toughest, we banded together," said sophomore offensive tackle Sam Young. "That's coaching. That's leadership. That's something we'll build from."

Each year, Notre Dame unveils "The Shirt," the official T-shirt that will dominate the student section that season. Clockwise from lower left are the 2006, 2007, and 2002 editions.

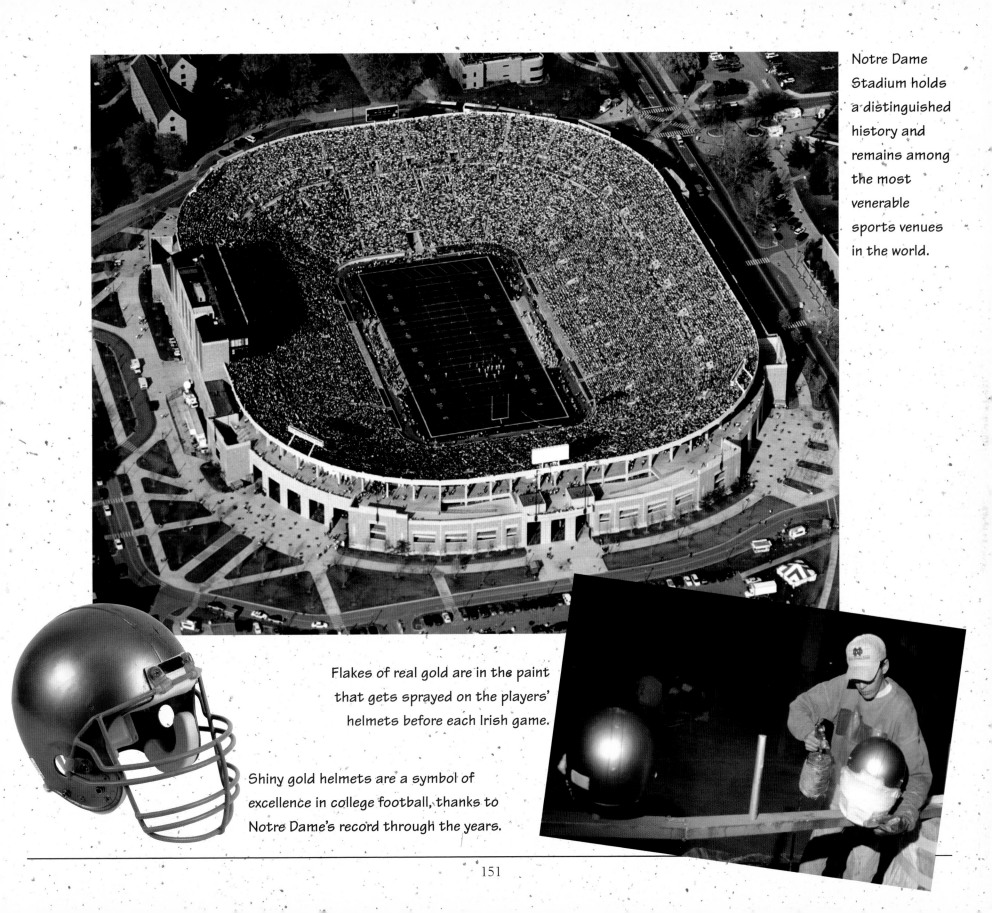

Notre Dame Stadium holds a distinguished history and remains among the most venerable sports venues in the world.

Flakes of real gold are in the paint that gets sprayed on the players' helmets before each Irish game.

Shiny gold helmets are a symbol of excellence in college football, thanks to Notre Dame's record through the years.

NOTRE DAME BY THE NUMBERS

Annual Records 1887–2007

Year	Coach	Record	Bowl	Year	Coach	Record	Bowl
1887	—	0–1–0	—	1913	Jesse Harper	7–0–0	—
1888	—	1–2–0	—	1914	Jesse Harper	6–2–0	—
1889	—	1–0–0	—	1915	Jesse Harper	7–1–0	—
1890	No Games			1916	Jesse Harper	8–1–0	—
1891	No Games			1917	Jesse Harper	6–1–1	—
1892	—	1–0–1	—	1918	Knute Rockne	3–1–2	—
1893	—	4–1–0	—	1919	Knute Rockne	9–0–0	—
1894	James L. Morrison	3–1–1	—	1920	Knute Rockne	9–0–0	—
1895	H. G. Hadden	3–1–0	—	1921	Knute Rockne	10–1–0	—
1896	Frank E. Hering	4–3–0	—	1922	Knute Rockne	8–1–1	—
1897	Frank E. Hering	4–1–1	—	1923	Knute Rockne	9–1–0	—
1898	Frank E. Hering	4–2–0	—	1924	Knute Rockne	10–0–0	Rose
1899	James McWeeney	6–3–1	—	1925	Knute Rockne	7–2–1	—
1900	Pat O'Dea	6–3–1	—	1926	Knute Rockne	9–1–0	—
1901	Pat O'Dea	8–1–1	—	1927	Knute Rockne	7–1–1	—
1902	James F. Faragher	6–2–1	—	1928	Knute Rockne	5–4–0	—
1903	James F. Faragher	8–0–1	—	1929	Knute Rockne	9–0–0	—
1904	Louis "Red" Salmon	5–3–0	—	1930	Knute Rockne	10–0–0	—
1905	Henry J. McGlew	5–4–0	—	1931	Hunk Anderson	6–2–1	—
1906	Thomas A. Barry	6–1–0	—	1932	Hunk Anderson	7–2–0	—
1907	Thomas A. Barry	6–0–1	—	1933	Hunk Anderson	3–5–1	—
1908	Victor M. Place	8–1–0	—	1934	Elmer Layden	6–3–0	—
1909	Frank C. Longman	7–0–1	—	1935	Elmer Layden	7–1–1	—
1910	Frank C. Longman	4–1–1	—	1936	Elmer Layden	6–2–1	—
1911	John L. Marks	6–0–2	—	1937	Elmer Layden	6–2–1	—
1912	John L. Marks	7–0–0	—	1938	Elmer Layden	8–1–0	—

Year	Coach	Record	Bowl	Year	Coach	Record	Bowl
1939	Elmer Layden	7–2–0	—	1974	Ara Parseghian	10–2–0	Orange
1940	Elmer Layden	7–2–0	—	1975	Dan Devine	8–3–0	—
1941	Frank Leahy	8–0–1	—	1976	Dan Devine	9–3–0	Gator
1942	Frank Leahy	7–2–2	—	1977	Dan Devine	11–1–0	Cotton
1943	Frank Leahy	9–1–0	—	1978	Dan Devine	9–3–0	Cotton
1944	Ed McKeever	8–2–0	—	1979	Dan Devine	7–4–0	—
1945	Hugh Devore	7–2–1	—	1980	Dan Devine	9–2–1	Sugar
1946	Frank Leahy	8–0–1	—	1981	Gerry Faust	5–6–0	—
1947	Frank Leahy	9–0–0	—	1982	Gerry Faust	6–4–1	—
1948	Frank Leahy	9–0–1	—	1983	Gerry Faust	7–5–0	Liberty
1949	Frank Leahy	10–0–0	—	1984	Gerry Faust	7–5–0	Aloha
1950	Frank Leahy	4–4–1	—	1985	Gerry Faust	5–6–0	—
1951	Frank Leahy	7–2–1	—	1986	Lou Holtz	5–6–0	—
1952	Frank Leahy	7–2–1	—	1987	Lou Holtz	8–4–0	Cotton
1953	Frank Leahy	9–0–1	—	1988	Lou Holtz	12–0–0	Fiesta
1954	Terry Brennan	9–1–0	—	1989	Lou Holtz	12–1–0	Orange
1955	Terry Brennan	8–2–0	—	1990	Lou Holtz	9–3–0	Orange
1956	Terry Brennan	2–8–0	—	1991	Lou Holtz	10–3–0	Sugar
1957	Terry Brennan	7–3–0	—	1992	Lou Holtz	10–1–1	Cotton
1958	Terry Brennan	6–4–0	—	1993	Lou Holtz	11–1–0	Cotton
1959	Joe Kuharich	5–5–0	—	1994	Lou Holtz	6–5–1	Fiesta
1960	Joe Kuharich	2–8–0	—	1995	Lou Holtz	9–3–0	Orange
1961	Joe Kuharich	5–5–0	—	1996	Lou Holtz	8–3	—
1962	Joe Kuharich	5–5–0	—	1997	Bob Davie	7–6	Independence
1963	Hugh Devore	2–7–0	—	1998	Bob Davie	9–3	Gator
1964	Ara Parseghian	9–1–0	—	1999	Bob Davie	5–7	—
1965	Ara Parseghian	7–2–1	—	2000	Bob Davie	9–3	Fiesta
1966	Ara Parseghian	9–0–1	—	2001	Bob Davie	5–6	—
1967	Ara Parseghian	8–2–0	—	2002	Ty Willingham	10–3	Gator
1968	Ara Parseghian	7–2–1	—	2003	Ty Willingham	5–7	—
1969	Ara Parseghian	8–2–1	Cotton	2004	Ty Willingham	6–6	Insight†
1970	Ara Parseghian	10–1–0	Cotton	2005	Charlie Weis	9–3	Fiesta
1971	Ara Parseghian	8–2–0	—	2006	Charlie Weis	10–3	Sugar
1972	Ara Parseghian	8–3–0	Orange	2007	Charlie Weis	3–9	—
1973	Ara Parseghian	11–0–0	Sugar				

† Ty Willingham was fired before the 2004 Insight Bowl. Kent Baer served as interim coach in that game.

Coaching Records 1887–2007

Years(s)	Coach	Record
1887–93	No coach	
1894	James L. Morrison	3–1–1
1895	H. G. Hadden	3–1–0
1896–98	Frank E. Hering	12–6–1
1899	James McWeeney	6–3–1
1900–01	Pat O'Dea	14–4–2
1902–03	James F. Faragher	14–2–2
1904	Louis "Red" Salmon	5–3–0
1905	Henry J. McGlew	5–4–0
1906–07	Thomas A. Barry	12–1–1
1908	Victor M. Place	8–1–0
1909–10	Frank C. Longman	11–1–2
1911–12	John L. Marks	13–0–2
1913–17	Jesse Harper	34–5–1
1918–30	Knute Rockne	105–12–5
1931–33	Heartly "Hunk" Anderson	16–9–2
1934–40	Elmer Layden	47–13–3
1941–43, 1946–53	Frank Leahy	87–11–9
1944	Ed McKeever	8–2–0
1945, 1963	Hugh Devore	9–9–1
1954–58	Terry Brennan	32–18–0
1959–62	Joe Kuharich	17–23
1964–74	Ara Parseghian	95–17–4
1975–80	Dan Devine	53–16–1
1981–85	Gerry Faust	30–26–1
1986–96	Lou Holtz	100–30–2
1997–2001	Bob Davie	35–25
2002–04	Ty Willingham	21–15
2005–07	Charlie Weis	22–15

National Championships

Notre Dame's 11 Consensus National Title Seasons

Year	Record	Coach
1924	10–0–0	Knute Rockne
1929	9–0–0	Knute Rockne
1930	10–0–0	Knute Rockne
1943	9–1–0	Frank Leahy
1946	8–0–1	Frank Leahy
1947	9–0–0	Frank Leahy
1949	10–0–0	Frank Leahy
1966	9–0–1	Ara Parseghian
1973	11–0–0	Ara Parseghian
1977	11–1–0	Dan Devine
1988	12–0–0	Lou Holtz

Notre Dame Bowl Game Record Won 13, Lost 15

Year	Bowl Game	Date	Opponent	W/L	Score
1924	Rose	Jan. 1, 1925	Stanford	W	27–10
1969	Cotton	Jan. 1, 1970	Texas	L	17–21
1970	Cotton	Jan. 1, 1971	Texas	W	24–11
1972	Orange	Jan. 1, 1973	Nebraska	L	6–40
1973	Sugar	Dec. 31, 1973	Alabama	W	24–23
1974	Orange	Jan. 1, 1975	Alabama	W	13–11
1976	Gator	Dec. 27, 1976	Penn State	W	20–9
1977	Cotton	Jan. 2, 1978	Texas	W	38–10
1978	Cotton	Jan. 1, 1979	Houston	W	35–34
1980	Sugar	Jan. 1, 1981	Georgia	L	10–17
1983	Liberty	Dec. 29, 1983	Boston College	W	19–18
1984	Aloha	Dec. 29, 1984	SMU	L	20–27
1987	Cotton	Jan. 1, 1988	Texas A&M	L	10–35
1988	Fiesta	Jan. 2, 1989	West Virginia	W	34–21
1989	Orange	Jan. 1, 1990	Colorado	W	21–6
1990	Orange	Jan. 1, 1991	Colorado	L	9–10
1991	Sugar	Jan. 1, 1992	Florida	W	39–28

Year	Bowl Game	Date	Opponent	W/L	Score
1992	Cotton	Jan. 1, 1993	Texas A&M	W	28–3
1993	Cotton	Jan. 1, 1994	Texas A&M	W	24–21
1994	Fiesta	Jan. 2, 1995	Colorado	L	24–41
1995	Orange	Jan. 1, 1996	Florida State	L	26–31
1997	Independence	Dec. 28, 1997	LSU	L	9–27
1998	Gator	Jan. 1, 1999	Georgia Tech	L	28–35
2000	Fiesta	Jan. 1, 2001	Oregon State	L	9–41
2002	Gator	Jan. 1, 2003	North Carolina St.	L	6–28
2004	Insight	Dec. 28, 2004	Oregon State	L	21–38
2005	Fiesta	Jan. 2, 2006	Ohio State	L	20–34
2006	Sugar	Jan. 3, 2007	LSU	L	14–41

Notre Dame Players in the College Football Hall of Fame

Year Inducted	Player	Position	Years Played
1951	George Gipp	HB	1917–20
1951	Elmer Layden	FB	1922–24
1954	Frank Carideo	QB	1928–30
1958	Harry Stuhldreher	QB	1922–24
1960	Johnny Lujack	QB	1943, 1946–47
1963	George Connor	T	1946–47
1965	Jack Cannon	G	1927–29
1966	Jim Crowley	HB	1922–24
1966	Edgar "Rip" Miller	T	1922–24
1968	Adam Walsh	C	1922–24
1970	Don Miller	HB	1922–24
1971	Louis "Red" Salmon	FB	1900–03
1972	Angelo Bertelli	QB	1941–43
1972	Ray Eichenlaub	FB	1911–14
1973	Leon Hart	E	1946–49
1974	Heartley "Hunk" Anderson	OG	1918–21
1974	Marchy Schwartz	HB	1929–31
1975	John "Clipper" Smith	OG	1925–27
1976	Creighton Miller	HB	1941–43

Year Inducted	Player	Position	Years Played
1977	Zygmont "Ziggy" Czarobski	T	1942–43, 1946–47
1978	Frank "Nordy" Hoffmann	OG	1930–31
1979	Johnny Lattner	HB	1951–53
1982	Bert Metzger	OG	1928–30
1983	Bill "Moose" Fischer	OG	1945–48
1983	Bill Shakespeare	HB	1933–35
1984	Emil Sitko	HB	1946–49
1985	Paul Hornung	QB	1954–56
1985	Fred Miller	T	1926–28
1987	Tommy Yarr	C	1929–31
1988	Bob Williams	QB	1948–50
1990	Wayne Millner	E	1933–35
1992	Jim Lynch	LB	1964–66
1993	Alan Page	DE	1964–66
1994	Jerry Groom	C	1948–50
1995	Jim Martin	E/T	1946–49
1997	Ken MacAfee	TE	1974–77
1999	Ross Browner	DE	1973, 1975–77
2000	Bob Dove	E	1940–42
2001	Ralph Guglielmi	QB	1951–54
2003	Joe Theismann	QB	1968–70
2005	John Huarte	QB	1962–64
2007	Chris Zorich	DT	1987–90

Heisman Trophy Winners

Year Won	Player	Position
1943	Angelo Bertelli	QB
1947	Johnny Lujack	QB
1949	Leon Hart	E
1953	Johnny Lattner	HB
1956	Paul Hornung	QB
1964	John Huarte	QB
1987	Tim Brown	FL

Consensus All-Americans

Year	Player	Year	Player	Year	Player	Year	Player
1913	Gus Dorais	1949	Leon Hart	1977	Luther Bradley	1989	Chris Zorich
1917	Frank Rydzewski	1949	Emil Sitko	1977	Ross Browner	1990	Raghib Ismail
1920	George Gipp	1949	Bob Williams	1977	Ken MacAfee	1990	Todd Lyght
1921	Eddie Anderson	1950	Jerry Groom	1978	Bob Golic	1990	Michael Stonebreaker
1924	Jim Crowley	1952	Johnny Lattner	1978	Dave Huffman	1990	Chris Zorich
1924	Elmer Layden	1953	Art Hunter	1979	Vagas Ferguson	1991	Mirko Jurkovic
1924	Harry Stuhldreher	1953	Johnny Lattner	1980	Bob Crable	1992	Aaron Taylor
1926	Art "Bud" Boeringer	1954	Ralph Guglielmi	1980	John Scully	1993	Jeff Burris
1927	John "Clipper" Smith	1955	Paul Hornung	1981	Bob Crable	1993	Aaron Taylor
1929	Jack Cannon	1957	Al Ecuyer	1987	Tim Brown	1994	Bobby Taylor
1929	Frank Carideo	1959	Monty Stickles	1988	Frank Stams	2002	Shane Walton
1930	Frank Carideo	1964	John Huarte	1988	Michael Stonebreaker	2005	Jeff Samardzija
1930	Marchy Schwartz	1964	Jack Snow	1989	Todd Lyght		
1931	Marchy Schwartz	1965	Dick Arrington				
1931	Tommy Yarr	1965	Nick Rassas				
1932	Joe Kurth	1966	Nick Eddy				
1934	Jack Robinson	1966	Jim Lynch				
1935	Wayne Millner	1966	Alan Page				
1937	Chuck Sweeney	1966	Tom Regner				
1938	Ed Beinor	1967	Tom Schoen				
1941	Bob Dove	1968	Terry Hanratty				
1942	Bob Dove	1968	George Kunz				
1943	Angelo Bertelli	1969	Mike McCoy				
1943	Pat Filley	1970	Larry DiNardo				
1943	Creighton Miller	1970	Tom Gatewood				
1943	Jim White	1971	Clarence Ellis				
1943	John Yonakor	1971	Walt Patulski				
1946	George Connor	1972	Greg Marx				
1946	Johnny Lujack	1973	Dave Casper				
1947	George Connor	1973	Mike Townsend				
1947	Bill Fischer	1974	Pete Demmerle				
1947	Johnny Lujack	1974	Gerry DiNardo				
1948	Bill Fischer	1975	Steve Niehaus				
1948	Leon Hart	1976	Ross Browner				
1948	Emil Sitko	1976	Ken MacAfee				

SCHOOL RECORDS & STATISTICAL LEADERS

Rushing Attempts

Game	40	Allen Pinkett vs. LSU, 1984 (162 yards); Phil Carter vs. Michigan State, 1980 (254 yards)
Season	301	Vagas Ferguson, 1979 (1,437 yards)
Career	889	Allen Pinkett, 1982–85 (4,131 yards)

Rushing Yards

Game	262	Julius Jones vs. Pittsburgh, 2003 (24 attempts)
Season	1,437	Vagas Ferguson, 1979 (301 attempts)
Career	4,318	Autry Denson, 1995–98 (854 attempts)

Games Rushing for 100 Yards or More

Season	10	Allen Pinkett, 1983
Career	23	Autry Denson, 1995–98

Rushing Touchdowns

Game	7	Art Smith vs. Loyola (Chicago), 1911
Season	17	Allen Pinkett, 1984; Vagas Ferguson, 1979
Career	49	Allen Pinkett, 1982–85

Pass Attempts

Game	63	Terry Hanratty vs. Purdue, 1967 (29 completed)
Season	467	Brady Quinn, 2006 (289 completed)
Career	1,602	Brady Quinn, 2003–06 (929 completed)

Pass Completions

Game	33	Brady Quinn vs. Michigan State, 2005 (60 attempts) Joe Theismann vs. USC, 1970 (58 attempts)
Season	292	Brady Quinn, 2005 (450 attempts)
Career	929	Brady Quinn, 2003–06 (1,602 attempts)

Passing Yards

Game	526	Joe Theismann vs. USC, 1970 (33 completed of 58 attempts)
Season	3,919	Brady Quinn, 2005 (292 completed of 450 attempts)
Career	11,762	Brady Quinn, 2003–06 (929 completed of 1,602 attempts)

Touchdown Passes

Game	6	Brady Quinn vs. BYU, 2005
Season	37	Brady Quinn, 2006
Career	95	Brady Quinn, 2003–06

Pass Completion Percentage (min. 10 completions)

Game	.909	Steve Beuerlein vs. Colorado, 1984 (10 completed of 11 attempts)
Season	.649	Brady Quinn, 2005 (292 completed of 450 attempts)
Career	.622	Kevin McDougal, 1990–93 (112 completed of 180 attempts)

Pass Receptions

Game	14	Maurice Stovall vs. BYU, 2005 (207 yards)
Season	78	Jeff Samardzija, 2006 (1,017 yards in 13 games)
Career	179	Jeff Samardzija, 2003–06 (2,593 yards)

Pass Receiving Yards

Game	276	Jim Seymour vs. Purdue, 1966 (13 receptions)
Season	1,249	Jeff Samardzija, 2005 (77 receptions)
Career	2,593	Jeff Samardzija, 2003–06 (179 receptions)

Touchdown Receptions

Game	4	Maurice Stovall vs. BYU, 2005
Season	15	Jeff Samardzija, 2005 Rhema McKnight, 2006
Career	27	Jeff Samardzija, 2003–06

Points

Game	37	Art Smith vs. Loyola (Chicago), 1911 (7 TDs worth 5 points each & 2 PATs)
Season	120	Jerome Bettis, 1991 (20 TDs)
Career	320	Allen Pinkett, 1982–85 (53 TDs, one 2-point run)

Touchdowns

Game	7	Art Smith vs. Loyola (Chicago), 1911
Season	20	Jerome Bettis, 1991 (12 games)
Career	53	Allen Pinkett, 1982–85 (43 games)

Field Goals Made

Game	5	Nicholas Setta vs. Washington State, 2003 (6 attempts); Setta vs. Maryland, 2002 (5 attempts); and Craig Hentrich vs. Miami, 1990 (6 attempts)
Season	21	John Carney, 1986 (28 attempts)
Career	51	John Carney, 1984–86 (69 attempts)

Consecutive Extra Points

Career	136	Craig Hentrich (from 9/30/89 vs. Purdue to 9/26/92 vs. Purdue; missed 2nd attempt vs. Purdue in 1992)

Interceptions

Game	3	by 13 players, most recently: Shane Walton vs. Maryland, 2002
Season	10	Mike Townsend, 1972 (39 yards)
Career	17	Luther Bradley, 1973, 1975–77 (218 yards)

Interception Return Yards

Game	103	Luther Bradley vs. Purdue, 1975 (2 returns)
Season	197	Nick Rassas, 1965 (6 returns)
Career	256	Dave Duerson, 1979–82 (12 returns)

Kickoff Returns

Game	8	George Gipp vs. Army, 1920 (157 yards)
Season	26	Julius Jones, 1999 (603 yards)
Career	72	Julius Jones, 1999–2001, 2003 (1,678 yards)

Kickoff Return Yards

Game	253	Paul Castner vs. Kalamazoo, 1922 (4 returns)
Season	698	Tim Brown, 1986 (25 returns)
Career	1,678	Julius Jones, 1999–2001, 2003 (72 returns)

Kickoff Returns for Touchdowns

Game	2	Raghib Ismail vs. Michigan, 1989; Raghib Ismail vs. Rice, 1988 Paul Castner vs. Kalamazoo, 1922
Season	2	Allen Rossum, 1997 Raghib Ismail, 1989 Raghib Ismail, 1988 Tim Brown, 1986 Nick Eddy, 1966 Johnny Lattner, 1953 Paul Castner, 1922
Career	5	Raghib Ismail, 1988–90

Punt Returns

Game	9	Tom Schoen vs. Pittsburgh, 1967 (167 yards)
Season	42	Tom Schoen, 1967 (447 yards)
Career	103	Dave Duerson, 1979–82 (869 yards)

Punt Return Yards

Game	167	Tom Schoen vs. Pittsburgh, 1967 (9 returns)
Season	459	Nick Rassas, 1965 (24 returns)
Career	947	Frank Carideo, 1928–30 (92 returns)

Punt Returns for Touchdowns

Game	2	Allen Rossum vs. Pittsburgh, 1996 Tim Brown vs. Michigan State, 1987 Vince McNally vs. Beloit, 1926
Season	3	Allen Rossum, 1996 Tim Brown, 1987 Nick Rassas, 1965
Career	3	Tom Zbikowski, 2004–07 Allen Rossum, 1994–96 Ricky Watters, 1987–90 Tim Brown, 1984–87 Nick Rassas, 1963–65

Punts

Game	15	Marchy Schwartz vs. Army, 1931 (509 yards)
Season	78	Joey Hildbold, 2002 (3,038 yards)
Career	259	Blair Kiel, 1980–83 (10,534 yards)

Punting Average

Game	51.9	Geoff Price vs. Michigan, 2006 (7 punts for 363 yards) (min. 5 punts)
Game	44.8	Paul Castner vs. Purdue, 1921 (12 punts for 537 yards) (min. 10 punts)
Season	45.4	Geoff Price, 2006 (50 punts for 2,272 yards) (min. 25 Punts)
Career	44.1	Craig Hentrich, 1989–92 (118 punts for 5,204 yards) (min. 50 punts)

All–Purpose Yards

(Yardage from rushing, receiving, and all returns)

Game	361	Willie Maher vs. Kalamazoo, 1923 (107 rushing, 80 punt returns, 174 kickoff returns)
Season	1,937	Tim Brown, 1986 (254 rushing, 910 receiving, 75 punt returns, 698 kickoff returns)
Career	5,462	Julius Jones, 1999–2001, 2003 (3,108 rushing, 250 receiving, 426 punt returns, 1,678 kickoff returns)

Total Yards

(Yardage from rushing, passing, receiving, and all returns)

Game	519	Joe Theismann vs. USC, 1970 (526 passing, 7 receiving, minus 14 rushing)
Season	4,009	Brady Quinn, 2005 (3,919 passing, 90 rushing)
Career	11,944	Brady Quinn, 2003–06 (11,762 passing, 182 rushing)

INDEX